Vol. 4 No. 3

Activate!

Music, Movement & More!

The Music Magazine for Grades K–6

Edited by Jeanette Morgan

Mission Statement

Heritage Music Press is proud to present this resource for all involved in teaching elementary students. We believe that music and movement are essential tools for learning and student achievement. It is our goal to present quality content that is developmentally appropriate, practical, and educationally sound. We strive to provide you with enjoyable opportunities to engage students in active learning.

HERITAGE MUSIC PRESS
Diverse Resources for *Your* Music Classroom
a Lorenz company • www.lorenz.com

Cover photo of Munich statues
© istockphoto.com/Achim Prill

From the Editor

Here it comes—winter—and do we ever have a snow-filled issue for you; snowflakes, snowmen, and sleigh rides, are all to be found in the following pages. We know how much kids love the winter and we want to bring that joy into your classroom.

I know that for most adults the winter is—well, how shall we say it—not so much fun. Who really enjoys trudging out to recess to spend 25 minutes in the freezing wind, constantly reminding the students to button up their coats (those crazy kids) and that throwing snowballs is against school policy? While we can't change the weather or the fact that you have to do recess duty, we can provide you with lessons and music that will bring some of that wonder back into the winter wonderland that you too once enjoyed. After all, this time of year really is wonderful. You've made it through the frantic first quarter, your concerts are around the corner, and by the end of the month you will have some well-deserved vacation time. When you come back in January, you've got a new year and a nice chunk of uninterrupted time for instruction.

Are you looking for a Kwanzaa piece, a Hanukkah piece, or how about a nice Christmas piece that isn't over the top? Well, you are in luck, we've got them all! This issue features four choral selections, and all of them can be modified to suit your needs. If you need to learn a piece in a hurry, just sing it all unison. If you have some time and/or a talented group of students, go ahead and add in the second part, the descant, the instruments, and the dance! From Jerry Estes's *Ragtime Holiday* to Brian Hiller and Don Dupont's lesson, *Noël Nouvelet,* we're spanning the centuries and musical styles.

With the combination of all of that singing and the chilly temperatures, your voice is probably beginning to feel a little ragged. If so, make sure to read Patricia Bourne's article on maintaining vocal health. As she suggests, it might be time to incorporate a few more listening and movement lessons into your instruction. No need to search too hard to find those lessons either; we've got them here too. Kate Kuper and Eric Chappelle have both contributed wonderful dance and movement lessons with super-cool recordings on the CD. Charlene Heldt presents two terrific listening lessons: *Sleigh Ride* for your little ones and *Hound Dog* for the older crowd.

And oh yes, I know what that last few days before vacation can be like, so we have included lots of games and activities to keep your students focused and give you a little breather without compromising musical learning.

All of us here at Heritage Music Press would like to wish you happy holidays and a prosperous New Year!

—*Jeanette Morgan, Editor*

Contributors

Blair Bielawski has an extensive and varied background in education. He holds a B.A. in Music Education from Carroll University in Waukesha, WI and an M.A. from the University of Wisconsin. He taught for twelve years at a variety of grade levels. Blair is currently an author and part of the advisory group for Lorenz Educational Press, along with being an author and composer for Heritage Music Press. An accomplished composer and arranger, Blair has over 70 compositions and arrangements in print, and his music has appeared in television shows and movies.

Patricia Bourne teaches K–6 general music, 5th/6th-grade chorus, and a 6th-grade marimba ensemble at Canyon Creek Elementary in Bothell, WA. A frequent guest conductor and clinician, she has served on the editorial committee of *General Music Today* and recently authored *Inside the Music Classroom: Teaching the Art with Heart*. Patty received her B.M.E. from Murray State University, M.M.E. from University of Oklahoma, and Doctorate of Education from Arizona State University.

Mark Burrows has written music and curriculum for numerous major publishers. His song collections, including the *Gettin' Down with Mama Goose* series and *Yo! Leonardo,* the first in his *Smarty Pants* series, top many best-seller lists, as do his percussion resources, which include *The Accidental Drum Circle* and *The Body Electric.* Known to many little listeners as "Mister Mark," he tours nationally, presenting high-energy family concerts. Mark received his undergraduate degree in music education from Southern Methodist University and his graduate degree in conducting from Texas Christian University.

Eric Chappelle, creator of the *Music For Creative Dance* series of CDs, has worked with Anne Green Gilbert at the Creative Dance Center in Seattle, WA since 1988 to provide focused and fun music for dance education. He recently produced *BrainDance Music*, a CD that introduces highly effective and flexible warm-up exercises based upon the developmental movement patterns that babies learn in their first year. In addition to his numerous residencies, Eric is a dance musician at Cornish College of the Arts and Dance Fremont in Seattle.

Don Dupont and **Brian Hiller** have more than 30 years of experience in music education. Currently teaching as music specialists in Westchester County, NY and professors at Hofstra University, they both have completed three levels of Orff-Schulwerk training and a master class. Together, they present workshops at national and state music conferences and have co-authored four publications: *It's Elemental: Lessons That Engage; It's Elemental 2: More Lessons that Engage; Earth, Water, Fire, Air: A Suite for Voices, Narrator and Orff Instruments;* and *Make a Joyful Sound* (Memphis Musicraft Publications).

Doug Edwards has taught elementary music for twenty years. An accomplished saxophonist and former middle and high school band director, Doug started a marimba ensemble at his school twelve years ago and quickly discovered how much elementary students could learn through an instrumental ensemble. Inspired, he began arranging and composing for marimba ensemble, and has been a presenter at local, state, and regional conferences. Doug holds a master's degree in education and currently teaches elementary music at Southgate Elementary in Kennewick, WA where he directs the Dragon Jam Marimba Ensemble and leads worship at his church.

Jerry Estes currently teaches vocal music at Wydown Middle School for grades six through eight. He received his B.M.E. with a vocal emphasis from Southwest Baptist University and his M.M. from Southern Illinois University. Jerry and his wife, Julie, have two children, Haley and Baxter.

Denise Gagné has taught band, choir, and classroom music from pre-school to college. Holding degrees in music and education, as well as certification in Kodály and Orff training, Denise is currently teaching music part-time and conducts the Red Deer Children's Choir. Her choirs and bands have won many awards at music festivals and have performed for local and national sporting events, on national radio, and even for the Queen of England. Denise has authored many elementary music publications including the *Musicplay K–6* textbook.

An experienced teacher with over 23 years in the field, **Charlene Heldt** currently teaches general music for grades K–6 and chorus for grades 3–6 in Gilbert, Arizona. She is also an online instructor for Grand Canyon University in Phoenix and has taught music courses for Arizona State University at the Polytechnic Campus. Charlene holds multiple degrees, including B.A. degrees in both Music Theory and Piano Pedagogy from Northeastern Illinois University and a M.M. in Music Theory from the Chicago Musical College of Roosevelt University. She has also completed her Orff Levels I, II, and III at Arizona State University.

Ingrid Hurlen is a well-loved teacher of creative arts, including dance, drama, music, and visual arts. She trained extensively with Anne Green Gilbert at the Creative Dance Center in Seattle, Washington and has taught there for twenty years. Her experiences also include teaching Using Movement, Music, and Drama in the Education of the Young Child at Edmonds Community College, performing with the family entertainment group The Tickle Tune Typhoon, and working as a Certified InterPlay® facilitator to mentor personal growth, creativity, leadership, and community building for adults.

Kate Kuper teaches creative movement to children, teachers, college students, and families. After working for several years as a professional choreographer, Kate shifted her focus and developed a concept-based approach to dance, focusing on preschool through eighth-grade children and inspiring thousands to move and learn. The author of four instructional audio CDs, Kate is also a Visiting Lecturer in the Dance Department at the University of Illinois at Urbana-Champaign and is a Workshop Leader for the Kennedy Center (Washington, D.C.).

Nicole LeGrand teaches K–5 general music at Madison Consolidated Schools in Madison, Indiana. Teaching at seven elementary schools, she works with over 1600 students each year. Nicole has 8 years of experience in the general classroom as an elementary teacher and three years of experience as the music specialist. She earned her Bachelor's Degree in elementary education from Hanover College. While there, she studied piano and served as one of the accompanists for the Hanover College Choir. She obtained her Master's Degree specializing in literacy from Walden University. She has directed both children's and adult's choirs in Madison. She also created and directs a fourth- and fifth-grade percussion ensemble at each of the seven elementary schools. Nicole has won vocal and instrumental awards and enjoys performing in many local venues.

D. Brian Weese has taught music in schools for seven years, during which time he has also served as music leader in churches. He has an undergraduate degree in Music Education from Grand Canyon University and a Masters in Church Music from The Southern Baptist Theological Seminary. Currently, he teaches Elementary Music in Walton County, GA.

Editors
Jeanette Morgan • Kris Kropff

Editorial Assistant
Jenny VanPelt

Design
Janine M. Chambers • Digital Dynamite, Inc.

Art Department
Patti Jeffers • Jeff Richards

Music Engravers
Jeanette Dotson • Linda Taylor

Recording Producer
Blair Bielawski

Activate! (ISSN: 1931-4736) is a periodical published bimonthly except June and July by Heritage Music Press, a division of The Lorenz Corporation, 501 East Third St., P.O. Box 802, Dayton, OH 45401-0802 (Ride-along enclosed). Periodicals postage paid at Dayton, OH 45401. **Prices**: $64.95 for an eight-month subscription (five issues); $124.95 for a two-year subscription (ten issues); $179.95 for a three-year subscription (fifteen issues). **Subscription prices include postage.** Please contact us for pricing for subscribers outside of the U.S. Individual issues are available for $19.95 each. Please notify *Activate!* and your postmaster when changing address. Allow four to six weeks for processing.

© 2009 Heritage Music Press, a division of The Lorenz Corporation. Some materials licensed from Themes & Variations and Ravenna Ventures. Some photos courtesy of Mark Mayberry. Images of Orff Instruments courtesy of Sonor (www.sonor-orff.com). Permission to photocopy the student activities and other reproducibles in this product is hereby granted to one teacher as part of the subscription price. This permission may only be used to provide copies for this teacher's specific classroom setting. This permission may not be transferred, sold, or given to any additional or subsequent user of this product. Thank you for respecting the copyright laws. Printed in U.S.A.

Postmaster: Please send address change to *Activate!*, P.O. Box 802, Dayton, OH 45401-0802.

To subscribe to *Activate!* or for other general inquiries, visit www.activatemagazine.com, call our customer service department at 800/444-1144 x1, or e-mail service@lorenz.com. Letters to the editor may be emailed to activate@lorenz.com or mailed to *Activate!* at P.O. Box 802, Dayton, OH 45401.

Contents

Ready, Set, Sing
Simple Songs and Activities

Ready, Set, Play
Songs to Utilize Classroom Instruments

Contents (continued)

Ready, Set, Move
Movement Activities and Teaching Strategies

Ready, Set, Learn
Lessons and Worksheets to Teach Music Terms and Concepts

The *Activate!* CD

The CD included with this issue is a mixed-media CD. It can be played in your stereo or CD player just like any "regular" CD, but it also includes data files that you can access through your computer. You will need the free Adobe Acrobat Reader to open these files. You may download it from www.adobe.com/downloads/. You'll find the Download link for Adobe Reader under "Players, readers and viewer." If you have any trouble accessing these files, please contact us at activate@lorenz.com.

All computers will behave differently depending on their individual settings. PC users who are *not* using iTunes as their default media player will likely get a pop-up with several options—in addition to Play/Import the CD using iTunes or Windows Media Player, there should also be an option to Open Folder to View Files. Selecting that option will display a list of all the files on the CD; you can open or print the pages you need from this list or save them to your local drive. If using iTunes, the CD will likely open in that program and ask if you want to import the audio files. If that's the case and you're a PC user, to access the file list you'll need to open Windows Explorer and click on the CD drive under "My Computer." Mac users will likely get two CD icons on the desktop—one for the audio files and one for the data files. Clicking on the data files icon will display a list of the files on the CD.

Audio Tracks

Here's an easy way to keep your *Activate!* CDs organized. Just photocopy and cut out this label and keep it with this issue's disc.

Corrections

In our August/September issue of *Activate!* there were some omissions and some corrections. We apologize and have included the omissions and corrected pages in this issue. You can find them in the Data Files on the mixed-media CD. We have also included a revised performance and accompaniment track for *Hop Old Squirrel* on tracks 30-31.

Data Files

The mixed-media CD with this issue includes:
- Lyric sheets for:
  - *Jamaican Noel*
  - *Ragtime Holiday*
  - *Matunda Ya Kwanzaa*
  - *Time for Hanukkah*
- Reproducible Recorder Scores for:
  - *Noël Nouvelet*
  - *God Rest Ye Merry, Gentlemen*
  - *Time for Hanukkah*
- Piano and Vocal Scores for:
  - *Jamaican Noel*
  - *Ragtime Holiday*
  - *Matunda Ya Kwanzaa*
- Visuals for:
  - *A Cold and Frosty Night*
  - *Noël Nouvelet*
  - *Hound Dog*
  - *Sleigh Ride*
- Additional Teaching Tips for *Beethoven's Funky Fifth*
- Reproducible Worksheets for:
  - *Musical Ornament*
  - *Candy Cane Caper*

August/September Corrections
- Ancient Egypt
- Respect Rap Visuals
- Boomwhacker Boogie, Boomwhacker Score

These materials are identified throughout the issue by our data files icon.

Activate! December 2009/January 2010 CD Tracks

Rock Around the Christmas Tree
1. Performance Track
2. Accompaniment Track

Jamaican Noel
3. Performance Track
4. Accompaniment Track

Ragtime Holiday
5. Performance Track
6. Accompaniment Track

Matunda Ya Kwanzaa
7. Performance Track
8. Accompaniment Track

Beethoven's Funky Fifth
9. Performance Track

Time for Hanukkah
10. Vocal Performance Track
11. Recorder Performance Track
12. Accompaniment Track

God Rest Ye Merry, Gentlemen
13. Performance Track
14. Accompaniment Track

15. *Rock 'n Stop*
16. *Action Dance*

Snowflake Dance
17. Step 1
18. Instrumental Only
19. Step 2, Melt and Pop Up
20. Melt and Pop Up Instrumental
21. The Snowflake Dance

Harmonious Holiday
22. *Jingle Bells*
23. *Deck the Hall*
24. *Greensleeves*
25. *Over the River*
26. *Good King Wenceslas*
27. *Up On the Housetop*
28. *We Wish You a Merry Christmas*
29. *Silent Night*

Hop Old Squirrel
30. Revised Performance Track
31. Accompaniment Track

December

Focus on Art Month
Hello Neighbor Month
Read a New Book Month
Safe Toys and Gifts Month
Universal Human Rights Month
Write to a Friend Month

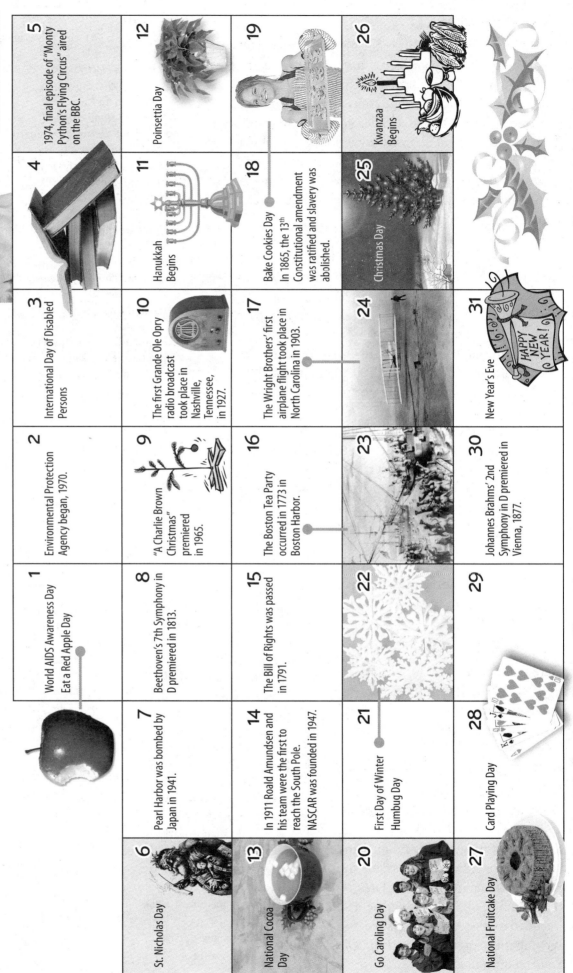

1 World AIDS Awareness Day
Eat a Red Apple Day

2 Environmental Protection Agency began, 1970.

3 International Day of Disabled Persons

4

5 1974, final episode of "Monty Python's Flying Circus" aired on the BBC.

6 St. Nicholas Day

7 Pearl Harbor was bombed by Japan in 1941.

8 Beethoven's 7th Symphony in D premiered in 1813.

9 "A Charlie Brown Christmas" premiered in 1965.

10 The first Grande Ole Opry radio broadcast took place in Nashville, Tennessee, in 1927.

11 Hanukkah Begins

12 Poinsettia Day

13 National Cocoa Day

14 In 1911 Roald Amundsen and his team were the first to reach the South Pole.
NASCAR was founded in 1947.

15 The Bill of Rights was passed in 1791.

16 The Boston Tea Party occurred in 1773 in Boston Harbor.

17 The Wright Brothers' first airplane flight took place in North Carolina in 1903.

18 Bake Cookies Day
In 1865, the 13th Constitutional amendment was ratified and slavery was abolished.

19

20 Go Caroling Day

21 First Day of Winter
Humbug Day

22

23

24

25 Christmas Day

26 Kwanzaa Begins

27 National Fruitcake Day

28 Card Playing Day

29

30 Johannes Brahms' 2nd Symphony in D premiered in Vienna, 1877.

31 New Year's Eve

January

3	4	5	6	7	1	2
J.R.R Tolkien's Birthday 	Trivia Day	National Bird Day	1759, George Washington married Martha Dandridge Curtis.	1992, AT&T released video-telephone ($1,499).	New Year's Day and Betsy Ross's Birthday	Musical "Hair" premieres in Amsterdam, 1970.

10	11	12	13	14	8	9
First Meeting of U.N. in London, 1946	Secret Pal Day	National Clean Off Your Desk Day	Make Your Dreams Come True Day		Elvis Presley Born in 1935	

17	18	19	20	21	15	16
	Martin Luther King Junior Day		2009, Barack Obama inaugurated as 44th President of the USA.	Pineapple introduced to Hawaii, 1813.	First Super Bowl played (1967). Green Bay defeated Kansas City, 35 to 10.	

24	25	26	27	28	22	23
National Compliment Day	"We Are the World" recorded in Los Angeles, 1985.		Wolfgang Amadeus Mozart's Birthday (1756)	1984, record 295,000 dominoes toppled in Fuerth, West Germany.	1859, Brahms' 1st Piano Concerto (in D minor) premiered in Hanover.	

31					29	30
Birthday of Franz Schubert (1797) and Philip Glass (1937)					1969, Jimi Hendrix and Pete Townshend waged a battle of guitars.	

ZSHC
HSKRN
CHKRVD
HONSDCV
OKHDNRCS
VHDNKUOSRC
BDCLKZVHSROA
HKGBCANOMPVESR
PKUEOBTVXRMJHCAZOI
DKNTWULJSPXVMRANCPGVZG

National Eye Care Health Month

National Oatmeal Month

National Thank You Month

Maintaining Your Vocal Health:

Care and Protection of the Music Teacher's Voice

By Patricia Bourne

In high school, and as an undergraduate, I played trumpet and ran on the cross-country team. Warm-ups were a crucial part of my daily routine, as hours of ensemble rehearsals were followed by hours spent running. Worn out "chops" were unacceptable. I understood the purpose of warming up, as well as the consequences of not. One would think that the act of warming up for any endeavor that exerted energy would be automatic, but that is simply not the case.

As an elementary general music teacher, talking and singing for hours replaced time spent blowing a trumpet and logging miles. The instrumentalist/athlete in me knew that a proper warm-up would ensure a better, healthier result, but that knowledge was set aside when I entered the classroom. After all, there were so many other tasks to accomplish before the kids walked in, and I was simply going to talk and sing; no big deal! Missing from my morning routine was the most important task necessary—a thorough and productive vocal warm-up.

According to Debra Spurgeon, "Music teachers are prone to experience voice problems because of the amount of speaking and singing required in the teaching day…" (*The Orff Echo,* Spring 2008). Most elementary general music teachers meet 8 to 10 classes a day, with rare opportunities for vocal rest. Without a proper warm-up, it's easy to see why so many music teachers face weeks of chronic laryngitis each and every year, reducing their speaking voices to painful squeaks.

For the last several years, I've had issues with laryngitis, particularly during the winter months. It troubled me enough to visit a laryngologist, who viewed my vocal folds through a fiber-optic laryngoscope. It was fascinating as well as revealing. Rather than the expected white color, my vocal cords were streaked with red lines, and rather than being of equal size, one was a good 1/3 larger. When I talked and tried to sing, the larger cord did not allow congruent vibrations to occur.

The good news: no permanent damage had occurred—yet. Acid reflux was diagnosed as the cause, and medication was prescribed to help. The outcome was positive, but more crucial was the realization that I needed to become more educated in order to protect and preserve healthy vocal cords.

Charles Peterson, a well-respected and brilliant vocal coach in the Seattle area, stated: "A proper warm-up is vital. There are two major muscle groups impacted in speaking and singing—those that control breathing and the vocal folds. An elementary music teacher will use his/her voice for 5–7 hours a day, five days a week. The demand on the voice is extraordinary" (Peterson, interview).

Another teacher, who experienced complete vocal cord shut-down stated, "I wish every college preparing music teachers would take the time to teach the importance and necessity to vocally warm-up each and everyday! I was an instrumental major who took voice class and sang in the choir, and although we

© 2008 Jupiterimages Corporation

warmed up, nothing was ever discussed about why or what particular warm-ups did to increase vocal stamina. I wound up not able to speak, so I went to a doctor and was told there was no significant damage to my vocal cords but was put on three weeks of vocal rest—as in, *no talking* whatsoever" (Stephanie Magnusson, interview). The culprit: too many hours of talking and singing throughout the day, too few water breaks, and a room not conducive to using a mild speaking voice.

Stephanie was given a prescription for vocal coaching, which led her to Mr. Peterson. After identifying factors that led to her vocal struggles, Peterson gave her a list of "must dos:"

- Warm-up everyday with a series of breathing exercises (diaphragmatic inhalation with exhales over an "f" sound with the teeth and breath); maintain one pitch (an e or f above middle c) using a long and forward "e" vowel; descending and ascending scales using each vowel sound; slightly accented and bouncy triads; and glissandos on an "o" vowel, starting with the lowest comfortable note and ascending to the highest comfortable note.

- Consciously raising the pitch of the speaking voice. When Stephanie began lessons, her normal speaking voice was an A below middle C—much lower than what was healthy for her.

- Frequently hydrate with water—sip early, sip often.

- Refrain from clearing the throat, as it pounds the vocal cords together.

- Strengthen lower abdominal muscles.

- Consistently get optimal hours of sleep per night.

Spurgeon suggests warming up the voice every day as well. "Exercises could include humming, yawn-sighs, tongue trills, arpeggios, and stretching, along with deep breaths to activate the abdominal muscles and prepare the teacher for the rigors of speaking and singing" (p. 31). She also invites those with the slightest beginning signs of vocal problems to:

- Make the teaching space as acoustically helpful as possible. Many teachers now employ amplification systems.

- Pay attention to the range of your speaking voice.

- Avoid singing with the students.

- Schedule speaking and relaxation breaks during the day. Stephanie adjusted her lesson instruction to include vocal breaks by incorporating more movement, more listening, and the use of a non-vocal quiet signal.

- Sip water throughout the day. "When our bodies are well hydrated, the mucosal lining of the vocal tract is slippery and this helps to minimize friction when we speak and sing and also reduces susceptibility to colds and sore throats" (Spurgeon, p. 33).

As a brass player and runner, I knew that resting my muscles was important. Likewise, my mentors instilled the habit of resting their voices when overly fatigued. Continuing to use the voice when it's fatigued is damaging the primary "tool" that elementary music teachers use in their teaching! "Think of a baseball pitcher. He will throw a game then rest for the next five days, allowing those critical muscles the necessary rest they need to rebuild." (Peterson).

While we certainly cannot rest our voices for several days, we can give it as much rest as possible, even while we are teaching. Peterson has found that many sufferers of chronic vocal fatigue have relied on "passive, everyday breathing" while teaching. Peterson advocates the use of "the kind of breathing and support that sustains [the] vital energy needed for high voice usage professionals."

In an effort to sustain my 28th year of teaching with optimum health and a robust voice, I'm taking Stephanie and Mr. Peterson's advice and will start by making time for an adequate vocal warm-up before students walk in. I can't wait to hear and feel the results!

References:

Magnusson, Stephanie. Interview by author on the phone, August 2009.
Peterson, Charles. Interview by author on the phone, August 2009.
Spurgeon, Debra. "The Music Teacher's Voice." *Orff Echo*, Volume 15, No. 2 (Spring 2008).

**Lesson suggestions
by Denise Gagné**

Target Concepts

Rhythm: Steady Beat
Form: AB
Tone Color: Classifying un-pitched percussion

Materials

- Recording of the song (performance and accompaniment)
- Non-pitched percussion instruments

Perf. **1**   Acc. **2**

Music-Making Activities

Singing
Playing instruments
Moving
Listening
Creating

Cross-Curricular Connection

Science: Classifying and organizing items by similar characteristics
Literacy: Creating new lyrics

Rock Around the Christmas Tree

Adapted by Ann Wood
Arr. by C. C.

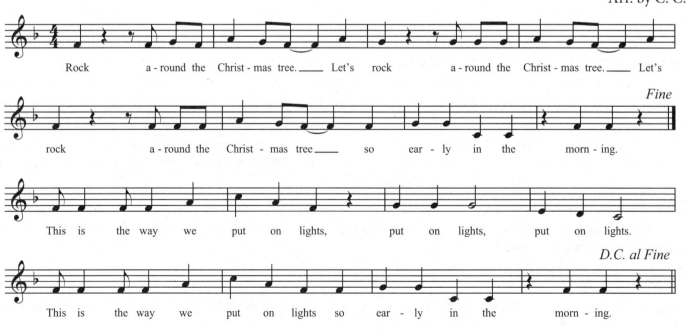

© 2009. Rock Around the Christmas Tree comes from the collection "Alphabet Action Songs" by Denise Gagné, and published by *Themes & Variations*. Visit www.musicplay.ca for more information on this collection.

Verse 2

This is the way we hang the bells, hang the bells, hang the bells. This is the way we hang the bells so early in the morning

Chorus

Verse 3

Put the star right on top, right on top, right on top. Put the star right on top so early in the morning.

Chorus

Suggested Process

1. Listen to the song, and ask your students questions about the music. For example:
   What is the song about? (Decorating a Christmas tree.)
   What are the singers in the song doing? (Putting on lights, hanging bells, putting a star on top.)

2. To illustrate the AB form of the music, invite the children to walk to the A Section and skip through the B Section. This will also help them to experience the different rhythmic figures used in the song. Invite the children to create movements to illustrate the lyrics. Ask them what kind of movements they might use for the chorus. Would they use different movements for the verses?

3. Invite the children to think of other things that they do when decorating a Christmas tree and create new verses. For example, "Hang some tinsel on the tree."

4. Change the words of the chorus to "Rock for the holidays, let's rock for the holidays, let's rock for the holidays so early in the morning," and have the children think of verses that could be used for other holidays that they celebrate.

5. Invite the children to choose non-pitched percussion instruments to play with the recording. When the children have chosen instruments, have them show you how they are held and played. Make sure that they are playing the instrument correctly. Listen to each of the instruments and classify them either by the way that they are played (tapping, hitting, shaking) or by the kind of sound that they make (wood, metal, shakes and scrapes, membranes).

6. Change the words of the song for the instruments. Have all the instruments play the beat or the micro-beat of the music during the chorus. During the verses, only selected instruments should play. Following are some possible verses and the new chorus. You will need to alter the rhythm to fit multi-syllabic instruments, like triangle.

Chorus:

Play for the holidays, let's play for the holidays.
Yes, play for the holidays so early in the morning.

Verses:

This is the way we tap the sticks, tap the sticks, tap the sticks.
This is the way we tap the sticks so early in the morning.

This is the way we shake the eggs, shake the eggs, shake the eggs.
This is the way we shake the eggs so early in the morning.

This is the way we play triangles, triangles, triangles.
This is the way we play triangles so early in the morning.

7. Choose three instruments to play for the final instrumental version. Perform this arrangement of the song using the accompaniment track or the piano accompaniment.

Rock Around the Christmas Tree

Adapted by Ann Wood
Arr. By C.C.

Rock a - round the Christ - mas tree.____ Let's

rock a - round the Christ - mas tree.____ Let's rock a - round the

Christ - mas tree____ so ear - ly in the morn - ing.

© 2009. Rock Around the Christmas Tree comes from the collection "Alphabet Action Songs" by Denise Gagné, and published by *Themes & Variations*. Visit www.musicplay.ca for more information on this collection.

This is the way we put on lights,
This is the way we hang on the bells,
Put_____ the star we right on the top,

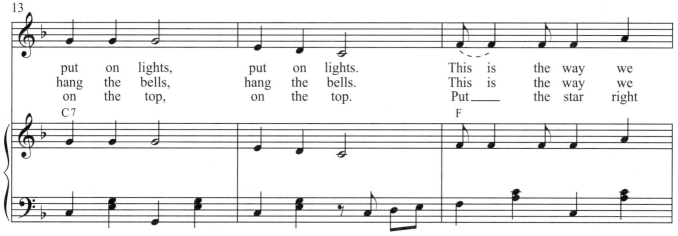

put on lights, put on lights. This is the way we
hang the bells, hang the bells. This is the way we
on the top, on the top. Put_____ the star right

C 7   F

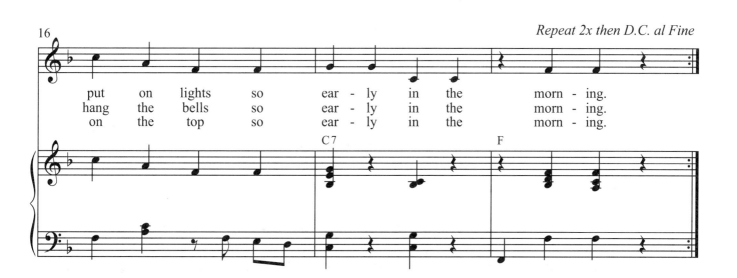

Repeat 2x then D.C. al Fine

put on lights so ear - ly in the morn - ing.
hang the bells so ear - ly in the morn - ing.
on the top so ear - ly in the morn - ing.

C 7   F

Jamaican Noel

Jamaican Folk Song

Adapted and arranged by Linda Spevacek

(Unison)
O can you feel the wonder and the magic out in the air?
   It's here! It's there! It's everywhere!
It has a feeling so contagious that your heart wants to sing,
   "Noel, noel noel."

Down in Jamaica, there is a song they sing all day long at Christmas.
If you go there you'll hear a beat and have happy feet, and dance.

(Part 1)
And you will feel the wonder and the magic out in the air.   It's here! It's there! It's everywhere!
(Part 2)   Sing,   sing and dance,
It has a feeling so contagious that your heart wants to sing "Noel, noel, noel."
(Part 2)   Sing,   sing "Noel, noel, noel."

When you go there you can join in the holiday fun at Christmas.
(Part 2)   ch ch   ch ch   ch ch   ch ch
Everyone can play instruments and play them Jamaican style.
(Part 2)   ch ch   ch ch   ch ch

"Noel, _____ noel, _____ noel. _____ Noel, __
   Oom pa tee chim chim, oom pa tee chim chim, oom pa tee chim chim, oom pa tee chim, chim
_____ noel _____ noel."
oom pa tee chim, chim, oom pa tee chim chim, oom pa tee chim, noel.

O can you feel the wonder and the magic out in the air? It's here! It's there!   It's everywhere!
   "Noel, _____ noel, _____ noel.
It has a feeling so contagious that your heart wants to sing, "Noel, noel noel, _ noel, noel, noel,
   Noel, _____ noel, _____ noel. Noel, _____ noel,
noel, noel, noel, _ noel, noel, noel!"
noel, _____ noel, noel, _____ noel!"

The original subscriber to *Activate!* has permission to reproduce this page for use in his or her classroom.
© 2009 Heritage Music Press, a division of The Lorenz Corporation. All rights reserved.

© 2008 Jupiterimages Corporation

Jamaican Noel

Jamaican Folk Song
Adapted and arranged by Linda Spevacek

The original subscriber to *Activate!* has permission to reproduce this page for use in his or her classroom.
© 2009 Heritage Music Press, a division of The Lorenz Corporation. All rights reserved.

*Add optional dance break to measure 53, choir turns and sways back and forth with 'touch step'.

Ragtime Holiday

Jerry Estes

The original subscriber to *Activate!* has permission to reproduce this page for use in his or her classroom.
© 2009 Heritage Music Press, a division of The Lorenz Corporation. All rights reserved.

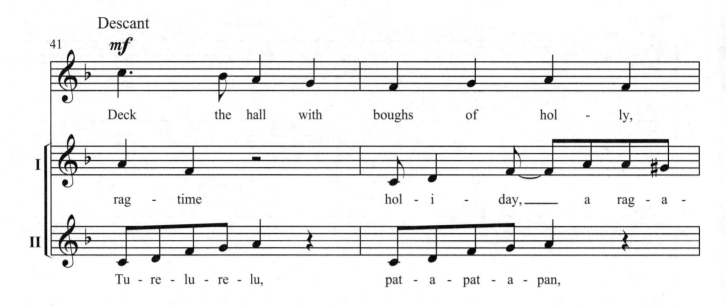

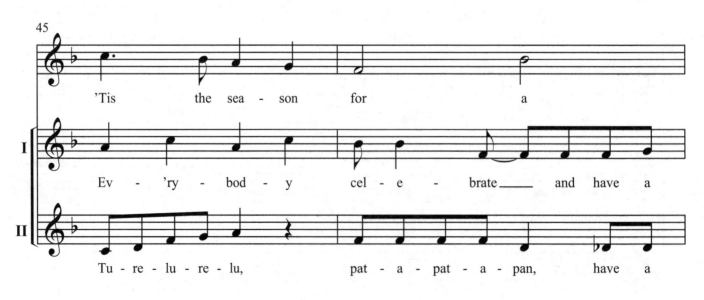

RAGTIME HOLIDAY

**Words and music by
Jerry Estes**

© istockphoto.com/Marcel Pelletier

(Part I and II)
Have a ragtime holiday, a rag a ragtime holiday.
   Everybody celebrate and have a ragtime holiday!

(Part I and II)
Deck the hall with boughs of holly, fa la la la la la la.
   'Tis the season for a ragtime holiday!

(Part II)
Have a ragtime holiday, a rag a ragtime holiday.
   Everybody celebrate and have a ragtime holiday!
(Part I) Deck the hall with boughs of holly, fa la la la la la la.
   'Tis the season for a ragtime holiday!

(Part I and II)
Tu-re-lu-re-lu pat-a-pat-a-pan, come be merry while you play.
Tu-re-lu-re-lu pat-a-pat-a-pan, have a ragtime holiday!

(Descant)   Deck the hall with boughs of holly, fa la la la la la la. 'Tis the season for a ragtime holiday!
(Part I) Have a ragtime holiday, a rag a ragtime holiday. Everybody celebrate and have a ragtime
   holiday!
(Part II)   Tu-re-lu-re-lu pat-a-pat-a-pan, come be merry while you play. Tu-re-lu-re-lu pat-a-pat-a-pan,
   have a ragtime holiday!

(Part II) Have a ragtime _____   ragtime holiday!
(Part I)   Have a ragtime_____ holiday!_____
(Descant)   Have a ragtime_____ holiday!_____

The original subscriber to *Activate!* has permission to reproduce this page for use in his or her classroom.
© 2009 Heritage Music Press, a division of The Lorenz Corporation. All rights reserved.

Matunda Ya Kwanzaa

Blair Bielawski

(Part 2)
First harvest, matunda ya Kwanzaa. First harvest, matunda ya Kwanzaa.

(Part 1 and 2 in unison)
First harvest, matunda ya Kwanzaa. First harvest, matunda ya Kwanzaa.

(Part 1 and 2 in harmony)
First harvest, matunda ya Kwanzaa. First harvest, matunda ya Kwanzaa.
We sing of fam'ly and faith. First harvest, matunda ya Kwanzaa.
We sing of unity and purpose. First harvest, matunda ya Kwanzaa.
We sing of creativity. First harvest, matunda ya Kwanzaa.

(Part 1 and 2 split)

Part 1	Part 2
We sing of fam'ly and faith.	**First harvest, matunda ya Kwanzaa.**
We sing of fam'ly and faith.	**First harvest, matunda ya Kwanzaa.**
We sing of fam'ly and faith.	**First harvest, matunda ya Kwanzaa.**
We sing of fam'ly and faith.	**First harvest, matunda ya Kwanzaa.**
We sing of fam'ly and faith.	**First harvest, matunda ya Kwanzaa.**
We sing of fam'ly and faith.	**First harvest, matunda ya Kwanzaa.**
We sing of fam'ly and faith.	**First harvest, matunda ya Kwanzaa.**
We sing of fam'ly and faith.	**First harvest, matunda ya Kwanzaa.**
We sing of fam'ly and faith.	**First harvest, matunda ya Kwanzaa.**
We sing of fam'ly and faith.	**First harvest, matunda ya Kwanzaa.**
We sing of fam'ly and faith.	**First harvest, matunda ya Kwanzaa.**
We sing of fam'ly and faith.	**First harvest, matunda ya Kwanzaa.**
We sing of fam'ly and faith.	**We sing of fam'ly and faith.**
Matunda ya Kwanzaa!	**Matunda ya Kwanzaa!**

The original subscriber to *Activate!* has permission to reproduce this page for use in his or her classroom.
© 2009 Heritage Music Press, a division of The Lorenz Corporation. All rights reserved.

Matunda Ya Kwanzaa

Blair Bielawski

Perf. **Acc.**

The original subscriber to *Activate!* has permission to reproduce this page for use in his or her classroom.
© 2009 Heritage Music Press, a division of The Lorenz Corporation. All rights reserved.

The Snowman Song

Lesson suggestions by Nicole LeGrand

Suggested Grades: K–2

Target Concepts

Melody: Contour, reading pitches E, G, and B on the treble staff

Rhythm: Half notes and half rests

Harmony: Combining pitches to create harmony

Materials

- A long piece of butcher block or bulletin-board paper (blue works nicely) or several sheets of 12" x 18" construction paper, taped together to create a long rectangle
- A black marker
- 4" white paper circles (25–30)
- Classroom instruments that can play the E, G, and B treble clef tones (xylophones, glockenspiels, resonator bars, handbells, etc.)
- 2"-tall by 4"-wide black rectangles

Music-Making Activities

Playing: Students will play instruments utilizing the E, G, and B treble-clef tones.

Reading: Students will read pitches E, G, and B and be introduced to the half-rest symbol.

Moving: Students will relate contour to movement with their bodies.

Creating: Students will create pieces of music utilizing half notes and half rests.

 Snowman Song Staff

Lesson Suggestions

1. On the blue rectangle (either bulletin-board paper or strip of taped-together 12" x 18" pieces of construction paper), draw three thick lines 4" apart, representing the bottom three lines of the treble clef.

2. At the left end of the paper, glue a white circle on each of the three lines and a black rectangle on top to create a "snowman." Put an E on the bottom snowball, a G on the middle snowball, and a B on the top snowball.

3. When the students arrive, ask them to tell you what they know about snowmen. You will get lots of answers. Show them the paper with the lines and the snowman, and ask them to tell you what they see. (three lines, three snowballs, a hat, the letters, etc.)

4. Bring out the instruments, and put a snowball with an "E" on the E tone, one with a "G" on the G tone, and one with a "B" on the B tone. Ask your students why they think you did that. Hopefully, they will make the connection between the letters on the snowman at the front of the room and the letters on the snowballs associated with each instrument.

5. Point to the E on the snowman, and play the E tone. Point to the G and do the same, and repeat the process for the B. Ask the students what they noticed about how the music sounded. Guide them to understand that as you went up the snowman from bottom to top, the music got higher. If they continue to have difficulties, start with the snowman's head and go down, each time pointing to the snowball and playing the sound. This might help your class to realize that as you went down the snowman, the sound also went down or got lower.

6. Take one of the blank white circles, and put it to the right of the snowman on the B line. Next, put one on the middle line. Then put one on the bottom line. Ask the students if the music will go up or down (down). Have them stand and reach for the sky when the snowball is on the top B line, stand with hands at their sides for the middle G line, and make a snowball with their bodies (crouch down) when the snowball is on the bottom E line. Using about six of the snowballs, create various patterns and have the students move to the music. Each time the students move to match the notes, play the corresponding note on the instruments. For example,

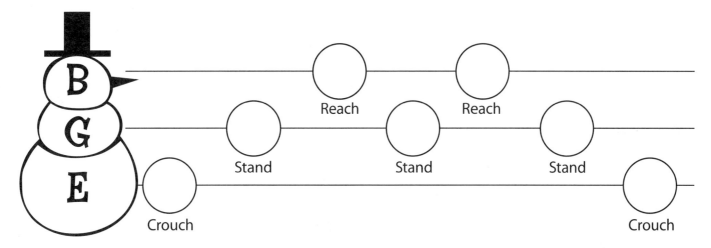

7. Tell your students that "The snowman's hat is a rest, which is a quiet time. The hat's name is a half rest." Be sure to emphasize how half and hat sound very much alike. Go on to tell them that "Each time you see a snowman's hat, you are going to count the numbers 1–2 in your head. Each time you see a snowball, we are going to let the sound play for a count of 1–2." Demonstrate these instructions for the students by putting a few snowballs and hats on the paper and then playing/counting the notes and rests together.

8. Choose students to come up, one at a time, and arrange the snowballs and hats on the lines. Then, let them play their creations. You can give your students paper and crayons to draw the last creation of the day on their own snowman staff.

Extension Ideas

- You can give your students the opportunity to revisit the lesson, this time stacking the snowballs on top of each other in various combinations to create harmony in their pieces. You would need to introduce the concept of harmony at the beginning of the lesson.

Assessment

Distribute a Snowman Staff, available on the mixed-media CD, to each child, instructing them to compose their own Snowman song. Once the students have finished composing, they can play it on a pitched instrument of their choice. As they are playing, assess their ability to play the correct pitch and/or duration.

A Cold and Frosty Night

Lesson suggestions and music by Patricia Bourne

Grade Levels: 3–4

Target Concepts

Melody
Rhythm
Tonality (optional)

Materials

- Copies of the song for each child, available in the Data Files on the *Activate!* CD
- Flashcards. These can be found in the Data Files on the *Activate!* CD.
- Bass xylophone, alto xylophone, alto metallophone, glockenspiel, soprano xylophone
- Various non-pitched classroom instruments

Music-Making Activities

Listening
Singing
Playing instruments
Reading notation
Expanding vocabulary

 Vocal Score

 Flashcards

Lesson Suggestions

1. Introduce the melody by singing it on a neutral syllable or playing it on a melodic instrument, such as the recorder. Always start at the beginning, but stop at different spots each time you play the melody.

2. As you sing/play the melody, your students should follow the sheet music and identify the specific places where you stopped by using the lyrics as a reference or using specific terms, such as, "In the third measure, second beat."

3. After hearing the melody several times, have your students sing the melody with the lyrics.

4. Ask the students to identify specific parts of the melody such as:

   "Which word has the highest pitch?"

   "Which measure has two half notes?"

   "Which measures show repeated tones?"

   These questions can be tailored to the concepts that you feel are most relevant to your class.

5. Demonstrate body percussion movements of your choice for each of the pitched instruments, and invite the students to sing the song while performing the body percussion. You may wish to introduce each pitched instrument in the following sequence: bass xylophone, alto xylophone, alto metallophone, glockenspiel, soprano xylophone.

6. As your students demonstrate proficiency in their ability to sing while performing the body percussion, transfer individuals to the pitched instruments, always solidifying each new part before introducing another.

7. Display the flashcards; the students should read the rhythms and then identify where that particular rhythm is found in the melody.

8. Transfer the flashcard rhythms to the non-pitched percussion instruments.

9. Once the full ensemble, with vocal line, is solid, you may choose to demonstrate how changing the melody to a major key alters the mood of the whole piece, thus introducing the idea of major/minor tonalities.

Extension Ideas:

- Sing the melody in a round.
- Challenge your students to create a form for the piece. Some ideas include having students choose the order in which the instruments should enter, when and how many times to sing the melody, or adding an Introduction and/or Coda.
- Provide empty snowflake rhythm cards and challenge your students to write alternative four-beat patterns that could be added to the ensemble.

© 2009 Heritage Music Press, a division of The Lorenz Corporation. All rights reserved.

Noël Nouvelet

Traditional French Carol

Lesson suggestions and arrangement by Brian Hiller and Don Dupont

---

Grade Levels: 4–6

Target Concepts:

Melody: Modes (Dorian)
Harmony: Singing simple chordal harmony
Form: AABA

Music-Making Activities

Singing
Listening
Playing
Dancing

 Noël Nouvelet fragments

 Noël Nouvelet vocal

 Recorder Score

Materials:

- Visuals of melodic motives, available in the Data Files on the *Activate!* CD
- Paper xylophone
- Orff instrumentarium
    BM: Bass metallophone
    BX: Bass xylophone
    HD: Hand drum, with mallet
    SM: Soprano metallophone
    SG: Soprano glockenspiel
    Triangle
    Soprano recorder (optional)
- Wrist bells (optional)

Noël Nouvelet is a melody written in the Dorian mode. This scale was used frequently in medieval times and is characterized by a raised-sixth scale degree (the Dorian 6th). Familiarize your students with the sound by playing a scale on the piano that begins with D and uses only the white keys, stepwise to the next D. The Dorian mode is considered ritualistic, religious, magical, and exalted. Note the absence of a key signature.

Lesson Suggestions

1. Present the following melodic motives:

2. Sing one of the motives on a neutral syllable (like "loo"). Have your students repeat the motive and then indicate the number of the motive by holding up the appropriate number of fingers. Repeat this procedure for the remaining motives. Challenge your students by having them lead the activity.

3. Combine the motives, and have your students identify the combinations. Finally, lead them to the following sequence: 1 2 1 2 3 4 1 2.

4. Familiarize the students with the following text. Speak in rhythm:

   Noël nouvelet, Noël chantons ici *(Noh-ehl noo-vehl-ay, Noh-ehl, shahn-tohns ee-see)*
   Dévotes gens, crions à Dieu merci *(Day-vo-tuh zhahn, kree-ohns ah dyuh mehr-see)*
   Chantons Noël pour le Roi nouvelet *(Shahn-ton Noh-ehl poor luh Rwah noo-vehl-ay)*
   Noël nouvelet, Noël chantons ici *(Noh-ehl noo-vehl-ay, Noh-ehl, shahn-tohns ee-see)*

5. Present the following visual:

6. Teach the melody with the text, echoing by phrases. Point out the form of the song (AABA). This is the form of many traditional French folk songs, such as *Au Clair de la Lune*.

7. Once familiar with the melody, have the students sing the i-VII chord roots (Voice 2). Divide the class in half. Have one group sing the chord roots as the other sings the song. Have the groups switch parts.

8. Prepare the orchestration through body percussion, text phrases, a paper xylophone, singing the pitches in rhythm, or a combination of all four methods.

9. Modelling good mallet technique, demonstrate how to play each instrumental part on its given instrument, choosing students to play each part as it is introduced and layering the orchestration as you progress until all instrumental parts are played securely.

10. Sing the song with the instrumental accompaniment.

11. Teach the following dance.

    Formation: Concentric circle of partners, each with wrist bells on the left hand

    Measures 1–4: Side R — close; Side L — close; Clap, pat (partner's hands), clap

    Measures 1–4: Repeat

    Measures 5–8: Right-hand palms touch, step the beat, and turn one time around (shake bells!)

    Measures 1–4: Side R — close; Side L — close; Clap, pat (partner's hands), clap

12. For the final performance, we suggest the following:

- Introduction: Orchestration (BX/BM/hand drum, Measures 1–4) 2x
- Sing the song with orchestration and dance.
- Interlude: Play the melody on the soprano recorder with orchestration and movement (omit low A). If you choose to do this, you may want to provide the recorder score to a small group of students so that they can practice prior to this lesson, or teach the recorder melody to your entire group in an earlier class.
- Sing the song with orchestration and dance.
- Coda: BX/BM/hand drum and wrist bells play, then fade out.

Extension Activities

Provide the following listening examples to further explore the Dorian Mode:

    Drunken Sailor
    Scarborough Fair
    She's Like the Swallow
    Eleanor Rigby (The Beatles)
    Ciacona in D (Johann Pachelbel)
    String Quartet in Dorian Mode (Ottorino Respighi)

Noël Nouvelet

Traditional French Carol

Arranged by Brian Hiller and Don Dupont

Noël nouvelet, Noël chantons, ici;
De - vo - tes gens, cri - ons a Dieu mer - ci.

Chan - tons No - ël, pour le Roi nou - ve - let,

Beethoven's Funky Fifth

Ludwig van Beethoven

Lesson suggestions and arrangement by Doug Edwards

Suggested Grades: 4–8

Target Concepts

Rhythm: Short-short-short-long pattern
Expression: Contrasting loud and soft
Style: Contrast Classical music with modern pop style
Vocabulary: *piano, forte,* and *crescendo*

Music-Making Activities

Playing instruments
Reading rhythm "eighth-eighth-eighth-quarter" pattern
Listening for dynamic changes

Materials

- Barred and varied percussion instruments
- A recording of *Beethoven's Funky Fifth,* arranged by Doug Edwards
- A recording of Beethoven's *Symphony No. 5, Movement 1* for orchestra
- Video of marimba performance by Southgate Elementary School Marimba band, Dragon Jam! Marimba band. www.teachertube.com or www.facebook.com/pages/Activate/4061473195 7?v=posts&viewas=1007182153

 9 Performance Track

 Teaching Tips

This well–known classical piece by Beethoven transcends time, continent, and age. More than likely, your students will recognize it within seconds of playing the famous opening motif. Though written hundreds of years ago for symphony orchestra, it still remains a favorite for people young and old. In terms of musical style, this arrangement melds the new with the old. While beginning in the original style of Beethoven, it quickly takes a two-hundred year leap forward to the modern style of pop and funk. From what we know about Beethoven's personality, I would guess that he might not approve of such a rendition; however, with all due respect to him, I think that your students and audiences will.

—*Doug Edwards, Arranger*

Lesson Suggestions

Students will:

1. If available, listen to a traditional recording of Beethoven's *Symphony No. 5, Movement 1* for orchestra, and participate in a discussion about what they know regarding the song and the composer. The instructor may wish to provide additional information.

2. Identify the four-note "short-short-short-long" rhythmic motif that is found in the opening measures. Discuss how Beethoven uses this pattern throughout the piece to guide his melodic ideas.

3. Listen for dynamic changes in the music and review/learn the terms *piano, forte,* and *crescendo.*

4. Listen to the recording of *Beethoven's Funky Fifth* and compare the differences between the original orchestral version and the pop version. Discuss these differences.

5. Learn to play the marimba parts found in Section A by rote learning.

Teaching Tips

- Teach the Orff parts two measures at a time. Once those measures are secure, teach the next two measures. Continue in this manner until the whole A Section is learned.

- Provide a beat for the students to hear while practicing their parts. I like to use a muted triangle sound. Mute the triangle with your fingers while hitting it with the beater.

- For more detailed instructional tips, see the additional resource file included in the data files on the *Activate!* CD.

Extension Ideas:

- Learn the marimba parts to the funky part of the arrangement—part B.

- Add a drum kit and other percussion instruments to the arrangement to help form the groove better (see resource file).

- Use the recording for performance ideas and layering ideas for the B Section.

To Bach and Beyond
Classical Works Creatively Arranged for Marimba or Orff Ensemble

Doug Edwards

Learning the classics just got a whole lot more fun! Teachers and students will have a blast with *To Bach and Beyond*, written by master music educator Doug Edwards. The musical arrangements are challenging but playable by upper level elementary-age students. Lesson suggestions guide the instruction, while invitations to adapt the material demonstrate Doug's understanding of both the classroom and elementary ensemble.

"I can't wait to hear my students tackle *Beethoven's Funky Fifth*, or *Für Elise Samba*! Creative, enjoyable, and learning-filled, these arrangements are sure to be a hit within the general music class or marimba ensemble."

—Patricia Bourne
Author and General Music Teacher

Beethoven's Funky Fifth (Beethoven) • *William Tell Overture* (Rossini) • *Minuet* (J.S. Bach)
Für Elise Samba (Beethoven) • *Russian Dance* (Tchaikovsky) • *The Wild Horseman* (Schumann)
Hallelujah Chorus (Handel) • *The Can-Can* (Offenbach)
Rondo Alla Turca (Mozart) • *Surprise Symphony* (Haydn)

30/2566H   Marimba or Orff Ensemble $16.95

Beethoven's Funky Fifth

Ludwig van Beethoven
Arrangement by Doug Edwards

Play "D" if the "B" is outside the range of the instrument.

© 2009 Heritage Music Press, a division of The Lorenz Corporation. All rights reserved. Printed in U.S.A.
Unauthorized reproduction of this publication is a criminal offense subject to prosecution.

Time for Hanukkah

Music by Mark Burrows

Lesson suggestions by Jeanette Morgan

Grade Levels: 3–4

Target Concepts

Melody: Playing high C

Materials

- Recorders
- Sheet music for each student or a way to project the music for your class
- Tambourine (optional)
- Performance and accompaniment recording tracks or piano score
- Visual of the lyrics (optional) included in the Data Files on the *Activate!* CD
- White board with staff lines

Music-Making Activities

Singing
Playing recorders
Listening/ear training

 Vocal Performance

 Recorder Performance

 Accompaniment

 Time for Hanukkah Lyrics

 Recorder Score

This lesson focuses primarily on melodic dictation. Before teaching this lesson, your students should have experience playing high C and echoing simple melodic patterns. If you would like, this music also lends itself well to introducing cut time.

Lesson Suggestions

1. Instruct the students to listen to this piece of music and be able to describe what they hear happening as the song progresses (it gets faster and faster). Play the performance track, or sing the song for the students as you accompany yourself on the piano.

2. Briefly discuss the *accelerando* and the Hanukkah holiday.

3. Teach the song by rote. Post or distribute the lyrics, if needed.

4. Once the students are secure with the song, instruct them to take out their recorders, and challenge them to figure out the melody for the first phrase. You may want to tell the class that the piece begins on pitch G. Allow the students several minutes to try to figure it out. Call on individual students to play the first phrase for the class, comparing and contrasting their versions to the original until the two match. Once you have established the pitches, have the entire class echo you or the student who correctly identified the melodic pattern.

5. Sing the next musical phrase for the students, and ask them what they notice about this phrase (it is the same melody as the first). Play the second phrase with the students.

6. Sing the third phrase and, once again, challenge the students to identify this melodic pattern. You may want to ask them to listen carefully to the starting pitch and identify it as higher or lower than the first pitch (G) of the earlier phrases (higher). Compare the sound of the pitch for "Time" with each note on the recorder, working your way up from G until they discover that it is a C. As before, allow the students to work out the rest of the phrase on their own.

7. Continue in this manner until the students have identified each phrase in the song.

8. Distribute, or project, the recorder music for this song. If you would also like to focus on cut time, this is a good point in the lesson to do so. Observant students may ask you about the time signature upon seeing the score.

9. Instruct the students to finger through the music as they listen to the performance track again.

10. Play along with the performance track.

11. Play with the accompaniment track, or better yet, accompany the class on the piano.

Performance Suggestions

- You can use this piece as a class or formal performance piece. Your students can sing the vocal line and then play their recorders during the repeats, or you could mix it up anyway you want! Have them play first, then sing—whatever works for you and your class. You can even have them arrange the performance as they like. Don't forget the tambourine part for added fun!

© 2008 Jupiterimages Corporation

Time for Hanukkah

Mark Burrows

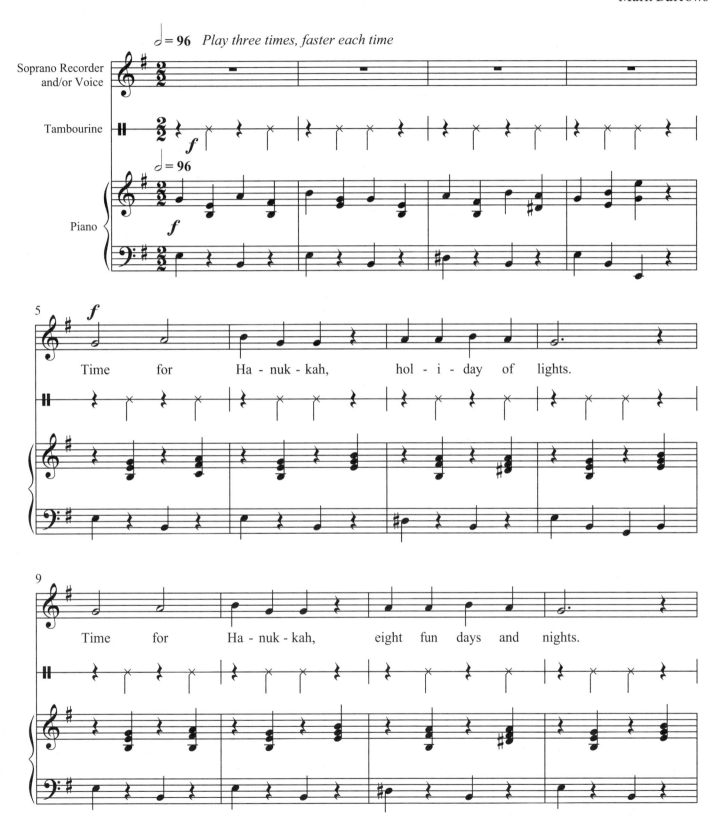

© 2009 Heritage Music Press, a division of the Lorenz Corporation. All rights reserved. Printed in U.S.A.
UNAUTHORIZED REPRODUCTION OF THIS PUBLICATION IS A CRIMINAL OFFENSE SUBJECT TO PROSECUTION

Time for Hanukkah

Mark Burrows

Voice/Recorder

The original subscriber to *Activate!* has permission to reproduce this page for use in his or her classroom.
© 2009 Heritage Music Press, a division of The Lorenz Corporation. All rights reserved.

Time for Hanukkah

Mark Burrows

Time for Hanukkah, holiday of lights.

Time for Hanukkah, eight fun days and nights.

Time for Hanukkah dance and sing and cheer.

Time for Hanukkah. Hanukkah is here.

Hanukkah is here. Hey!

The original subscriber to *Activate!* has permission to reproduce this page for use in his or her classroom.
© 2009 Heritage Music Press, a division of The Lorenz Corporation. All rights reserved

GOD REST YE MERRY, GENTLEMEN

Lesson suggestions by Jeanette Morgan

Arrangement by Blair Bielawski

Suggested Grade Levels: 4–6

Target Concepts

Melody: playing high E
Rhythm: syncopation
Harmony: duet
Form: AABC
Style: Jazz

Perf. (13)   Acc. (14)

Materials

- Sheet music for *God Rest Ye Merry, Gentlemen*
- Performance and accompaniment recordings

Music-Making Activities

Reading music
Playing the recorder
Listening
Improvisation

I love this traditional melody and am excited to present Blair's updated jazzy rendition. I know that many of us stay away from pieces that feature high E and cringe at the thought of hearing the upper registers of the recorder, but this piece does feature that very note. Make sure to introduce the pitch with a good quality yourself and insist that the students do the same. If you just can't stand the sound of the high E, feel free to substitute a C instead. You may want to begin class by having your students echo some simple melodic passages that feature syncopation, e-minor tonality, and that dreaded high E!

Lesson Suggestions

1. Instruct your students to listen to this holiday melody and identify the following two things: the title of the piece and the form (AABC). If your students are not familiar with the term "form," ask them to identify the number of sections that they hear in this melody (four). Using good tone quality and playing technique, play the opening melody of the piece through measure 21. You may have to play it several times for your students to identify the form. You may also assist the students by asking them to compare/contrast each section and thus discover that they hear the A Section two times.

2. Once the title and form have been identified, distribute or project the sheet music. Work slowly through the piece, learning each section before proceeding to the next. You may wish to have students work on their own, in small groups, or learn through a combination of reading the music and rote as guided by you.

3. Discuss/review the term syncopation. Clap the syncopated rhythm found in measure 23, indicating that your students should echo you. Instruct your students to locate all of the places that they see a syncopated rhythm in the music. Play through each of these passages to prepare students for playing the jazz arrangement.

4. Instruct your students to listen to the performance recording while they finger along with the music.

5. Play along with the performance recording and then the accompaniment recording.

Extension Activity

- Using other holiday melodies, challenge your students to create jazzy variations on the original melody, as has been done in this piece.

GOD REST YE MERRY, GENTLEMEN

Recorder

Traditional
Arr. by Blair Bielawski

The original subscriber to *Activate!* has permission to reproduce this page for use in his or her classroom.
© 2009 Heritage Music Press, a division of The Lorenz Corporation. All rights reserved.

Snowflake Dance

Lesson suggestions by Kate Kuper

Suggested Grades: K–2

Target Dance Concepts

Moving with expressive qualities
Listening and responding to words and sound
  sources
Making body shapes
Performing changes of level (high and low), flow
  (free and bound), and speed (fast and slow)

Materials:

- Recordings of *Action Dance* and *Snowflake Dance*
- Drum or other hand-held instrument
- Pictures of snowflakes (Paper snowflakes mounted on black paper work nicely.)
- Examples of lace filigree
- Large, open space suitable for movement

Music-Making Activities

Listening and responding to music
Moving to music
Cross-curricular focus
Language arts

 Action Dance

 Snowflake Dance

The following lesson suggestions are designed for a four-week unit. Each lesson builds on the experiences from the previous class period. Of course, depending on the length of your class and the time that you have available to teach this lesson, you can teach it as presented here or in one or two longer periods.

Lesson Suggestions

Week 1

- Present the following words to your class: float, melt, explode, twirl, spin, and whirl. Discuss these words with your students, and either demonstrate using your body to express these action words or ask student volunteers to do so.

- Perform *Action Dance* with your students. You may want to listen and practice your movements before you present this dance to the class. You can also see a video of this dance by visiting the following site: www.facebook.com/pages/Activate/40614731957?v=posts&viewas=1007182153

- Return to a seated position, and instruct your students to listen as you read the following poem. As they are listening, they should think about a potential title for this poem and pay attention to any words that they may not already know.

- Read the poem *The Snowflake* by Walter de la Mare.

The Snowflake

By Walter de la Mare

Before I melt,
Come, look at me!
This lovely icy filigree!
Of a great forest
In one night
I make a wilderness
Of white:
By skyey cold
Of crystals made,
All softly, on
Your finger laid,
I pause, that you
My beauty see:
Breathe; and I vanish
Instantly.

Used by permission of The Literary Trustees of Walter de la Mare and
The Society of Authors as their representative. Public Performance Rights Reserved.

- Discuss the following questions with your class:

    What is this poem about?

    What would be a good title for this poem?

    What is "filigree?" (Show examples):

    Why does the poet compare snowflakes to filigree?

    What does "pause" mean? "Vanish?" "Crystal?"

- Instruct the students to spread out in the classroom space, sitting in the ready position (establish what this looks like before you begin), and facing you.

- Discuss snowflake shapes: spiky, symmetrical (matching shapes), and linear. Have your students use their bodies to make snowflake shapes. Encourage a variety of choices and express your observations.

- Instruct your students to change their snowflake shape every time they hear your cue. Using a drum or hand-clap, play a double-beat cue to signal changes between different types of snowflakes because "no two snowflakes are alike!"

- Sitting in the ready position, discuss what happens when snow melts. What shape does it become? (A round drop)

- Instruct the students to stand up and freeze in their snowflake shapes. Tell them that when you say "I breathe on you, and you melt," they should melt to the ground, and when you say "Pop up!" they should return to a new snowflake shape. Repeat this activity several times. You may have to remind your class to keep their feet under them, even though they are low and closed, so that they can pop up again quickly and smoothly.

Week 2

- Review the snowflake melting and pop-up activity from last week either by discussing it or quickly revisiting the activity.

- With the class in a seated, ready position, ask them "How does snow move, when blown by the wind?" Take several suggestions, leading them to the action words of "swirl," "float," and "twirl." Discuss and demonstrate these actions.

- Instruct your students to move in their spots as you call out "swirl," "float," or "twirl," cuing a "freeze" between each action. The cue can be verbal or using a simple percussion instrument.

- Divide the class into groups of five to seven students. The groups do not have to sit together. If you prefer, they can be scattered throughout the room.

- Using the rhyme below, demonstrate how to move through the room like snowflakes. The students will move away from their spots for eight beats, freeze for four beats, and then move back to their spots for another eight beats. Demonstrate and encourage them to use a different pathway to and from their spots.

"Swirl and twirl a-round you go, and now you're going to stop like snow. (8 beats)
FREEZE! (4 beats)
Swirl and twirl and go back home, and now you will no longer roam. (8 beats)
Freeze upon your spot, and now you may sit down." (4 beats)

- Review the words "pause," "breathe," and "vanish." What do they mean? What happens if you breathe on a snowflake? (It melts).

- Repeat the traveling movement as before, but use this rhyme instead:

    "Swirl and twirl around you go, and now you're going to stop like snow. (8 beats)
    Pause. (4 beats)
    Melt down. (4 beats)
    Pop up! (4 beats)
    Now vanish! (As a 2 beat pick up before the next "swirl" phrase)
    Swirl and twirl and go back home, and now you will no longer roam. (8 beats)
    Freeze upon your spot." (4 beats)

Week 3

- Quickly review the movement activity from the previous lesson.

- Introduce the drum cues that you will use today in place of words. Instead of saying the poem, the class will hear the following cues:

  "Swirl and twirl" is played as an uneven, skipping beat.

  "Freeze" is cued by a strong single beat.

  "Melt down" is cued by a continuous, steady, soft pulse.

  "Pop up!" is cued by a strong double beat.

  "Swirl and twirl" is played again as an uneven beat.

  "Freeze upon your spot" is cued by a strong single beat.

  "And now you may sit down" is cued by a new sound. (I use the jingles on the side of my tambourine for this and play the side of my tambourine with a stick for "melt down.")

- Perform the movement activity using the drum cues and continuing to encourage your students to move in different ways, using different pathways and levels.

- Instruct the students to sit in a large circle

- Demonstrate the idea of group shapes by using five to seven children as your models.

- The model group stands, and, **one by one**, group members swirl and twirl to the center of the circle, <u>in the pathway of their choice</u>, freezing in snowflake shapes using the same rhythm as earlier in the lesson. You can establish the order in which the students move before beginning the activity, or you can simply point to or gently tap the next dancer.

- As each new member joins the snowflake shape, they must add on to the shape, either by connecting in at least one place or by filling in spaces (negative space) in the shape.

Here are some things to keep in mind when making group shapes:

Shape: Spiky, radiating out like the rays of the sun, symmetrical, etc.

Variety: Do different things each time because no two snowflakes are alike!

Avoid making "paper dolls" by just adding on to either end of a shape; look for other choices.

Try high and low shapes; wide and narrow shapes.

Support any parts that need supporting (like a leg, arm, or back).

Do not press down on anyone in the shape. This is not a football pile up!

When everyone is in the shape, they "pause."

- The words, "I breathe on you and you melt" melts the whole group down.

- On the word "vanish," combined with the "pop-up!" the whole group pops up to the shape that it was in before the "melt."

- On the word "instantly," combined with the "swirl and twirl" uneven beat, everyone swirls and twirls back to their standing spot on the circle.

- Cue "stop" and "sit."

- Repeat this procedure with each group, letting the drum do the talking.

Week 4 (Final Performance)

- Seated in a large circle, reread *The Snowflake*. Discuss all of the ways that the class has moved like snowflakes. Be sure to emphasize the individual movements and the group shape.
- Divide the class into groups of six dancers. Assign each dancer a line in the poem, and/or number, so that they will know who should move and when.

Text	Movement	Beats
"Before I melt, Come look at me!"	First dancer "swirls and twirls" to the center and freezes.	8
"This lovely icy filigree!"	Second dancer "swirls and twirls" to the center and freezes, attaching to the first dancer to begin the group shape.	8
Of a great forest In one night"	Third dancer "swirls and twirls" to center and freezes, attaching to the group shape.	8
"I make a wilderness Of white:"	Fourth dancer "swirls and twirls" to the center and freezes, attaching to the group shape.	8
"By skyey cold Of crystals made,"	Fifth dancer "swirls and twirls" to the center and freezes, attaching to the group shape.	8
"All softly, on Your finger laid,"	Sixth dancer "swirls and twirls" to the center and freezes, attaching to the group shape.	8
"I pause, that you My beauty see:"	The group holds the shape.	4
"Breathe;"	The group melts.	4
"and I vanish,"	The group pops up.	4
"Instantly"	The group disperses, "swirling and twirling" back to their original spots, while the teacher plays the rhythm on the drum to accompany this movement.	8

Closure:

- In a seated circle, discuss the following questions:

  How did your group make snowflake shapes?
  How did you travel to the shape?
  How did your group know when to melt?
  How did your group know when to travel back to the circle?

Rock 'n Stop

Lesson suggestions by Ingrid Hurlen

Music by Eric Chappelle

Grades Pre-K–4

Target Concepts

Rhythm: Playing and moving to the steady beat

Materials:

- Non-pitched classroom instruments
- A recording of *Rock 'n Stop*

Movement Concepts

Place: Self-space and general space, moving in different directions, levels in space, pathways or big/little movements.

Speed: Rhythm and tempo

Music-Making Activities

Listening
Playing instruments
Moving to music

Summary

Using rhythm instruments, the students will play a steady beat along with the tempo of the music. Then, students will move freely while improvising their own rhythms.

Lesson Suggestions

1. Have your students stand back-to-back with a partner.

2. On a classroom instrument of your choice, demonstrate a steady beat while you bend your knees to the pulse of the music.

3. Distribute rhythm instruments to your students, and instruct them to continue standing back-to-back with their partners. The students should play the steady beat and bend their knees along with that beat. When the music pauses, stop.

4. Next, have the students move through the classroom space, playing their own rhythm with the next section of music. You may have to demonstrate this and stress that the students should make up their own rhythm to play rather than copying yours.

5. Continue moving and playing to the music, alternating playing a steady beat with a partner with moving and improvising a rhythm.

6. Challenge your students to move in different directions, levels in space, pathways (curved, straight, zigzag), and/or with little or big movements. Demonstrate each of these concepts, and help your students to remember your instructions by calling out suggestions or questions that will engage them in their movements. For example, you could say, "Can you move backwards?"

Variations

- For younger students, instead of having partners, lead the steady beat with the whole group. Suggest different ways of moving freely and playing alternately with each section of music.

- When the music stops, freeze in a shape and try balancing. When the music resumes, change your level or direction of movement; the next time you freeze, balance on a different body part.

- Shadow or mirror movements with a partner. One student should be the leader while the other follows. When the music pauses, change leaders.

Hound Dog

Music by Jerry Leiber and Mike Stoller

Lesson suggestions by Charlene Heldt

Grade Levels: 3–6

Target Concepts

Form: 12-bar blues
Rhythm: Syncopation

Materials

- Pitched and non-pitched classroom instruments
- Recordings of *Hound Dog* performed by Elvis and Big Mama Thornton.
- Guided listening worksheets for your students
- A visual representation of the chord structure of *Hound Dog*. Visuals are provided in the Data Files on the *Activate!* CD.

Music-Making Activities

Listening
Playing
Creating

 Guided Listening Worksheet

 Hound Dog Visuals

Lesson Suggestions: Two Class Periods

Lesson 1:

1. Before your students arrive, prepare by choosing your favorite Elvis song (other than *Hound Dog*) and queuing a recording to play as they enter the room.

2. Once the students are seated, ask if they could identify the singer and song.

3. Ask students to share any and all information that they know about Elvis Presley.

4. Share basic information about Elvis:
   - He is known as the "King of Rock 'n Roll."
   - Elvis Aaron Presley was born on January 8, 1935 in Tupelo, Mississippi.
   - He died on August 16, 1977 at the age of 42.
   - He was discovered when he went to make a demo record at Sun Records in Memphis, Tennessee.
   - Elvis starred in numerous films and appeared on television many times.

5. Instruct the students to listen and identify the title of this well-known Elvis song. Play the first minute of Elvis's version of *Hound Dog*.

6. Ask your students to think about the text of this song, and discuss the meaning of these words. You may need to play it again, stopping for discussion after each phrase.

7. Ask the class to think about where Elvis (or any singer) may have gotten his ideas. As the discussion progresses, introduce Big Mama Thornton as a Rhythm and Blues singer whose biggest hit was *Hound Dog*, written by Leiber and Stoller in 1952. It would be beneficial to relate the idea of re-makes to a current artist.

8. Instruct the students to listen to Big Mama Thornton's version of the same song. Very briefly, discuss some of the obvious similarities and differences.

9. Distribute the Guided Listening Worksheets (two per child or group, one for each version), and have students complete them either individually or in small groups. You will probably have to play each example several times in its entirety.

10. Once the class has finished the Guided Listening Worksheets, have them assemble on the floor in front of your white board and construct a Venn Diagram.

11. Close the lesson by holding a vote to see which version the class prefers. Post results from the poll in your hallway so that other classes can see the results and, hopefully, discuss them.

Lesson 2

1. Review key points from the previous lesson.

2. Define the 12-bar blues form. Listen to *Hound Dog* again, identifying the three phrases: A A B. Explain to students that this form is often described as a question, question, and an answer or a statement, statement, and closing form. Whichever description you prefer to use is fine.

3. Help the students to identify these phrases in the lyrics as they listen to one version of *Hound Dog*. If you feel that your students need more support in learning this concept, complete the 12-Bar Movement Blues activity in the Extension Activities before continuing with the lesson. You can also have the class compose their own Blues lyrics based on the form of *Hound Dog*, as suggested below.

4. Using the visual of the chord structure, explain the typical chord progressions for 12-bar blues. Play the progression on the piano or barred instrument of your choice while having the students follow along with the visual.

5. Discuss the chord names, roman numerals, and terms associated with each chord (tonic, dominant, subdominant).

6. Listen to *Hound Dog* by Elvis as you point to the chord labels. You may wish to repeat this activity, having a student point to the visual as they are listening or having students hold up fingers to indicate the chord that they are hearing.

7. Depending on your students' proficiency, choose one of the two playing options below.

Option 1 (Easy)
- Set up the instruments in the following manner:
  Bass Xylophone: Have only pitch C on the instrument.
  Alto Xylophones: Have only pitch F on the instrument.
  Sopranos Xylophones: Have only pitch G on the instrument.
- Post or project the *Hound Dog* chord visual using the Roman numeral chord symbols.
- While playing the recording of *Hound Dog* by Elvis, have the students play the appropriate chord root. Use two students per instrument, one per root (i.e. C, F, or G). Instruct the students to change instruments between verses in a round-robin manner, resulting in their playing each different chord root and instrument.
- Repeat as needed to allow all students the chance to play.
- A teacher or a student may need to point to or say the chord progression to keep everyone on track.

Option 2

- Set up the instruments in the following manner:
  - Bass Xylophone: C chord (C, E, G)
  - Alto Xylophones: F chord (F, A, C)
  - Sopranos Xylophones: G chord (G, B, D)
- Post or project the chord structure, using the pitch names and chord roots.
- Assign one student to each chord pitch, three students per instrument. For example, one student should play C, another plays E, and the last of the three plays G for the C Chord. You could also have your students use double mallets with one hand so that each may play a full chord. This option is great for a really talented bunch!
- Play the recordings, and have students play the full chords following the chart on the board.
- A teacher or a student may need to point to or say the chord progression to keep everyone on track.

8. To close the lesson, ask your students to recall all that they have learned about the blues in the last two classes, and make a list on the board to summarize their learning.

Extension Activities

- Have your students compose their own lyrics in the Statement/Statement/Closure or Question/Question/ Answer form of the 12-bar blues. For example, "I don't know a thing about the blues. No, I don't know a thing about the blues. Well, now I do, and so can you!" or "What are we learning today? I said, what are we learning today? We're learning about the blues, the good ol' fashioned way!"

- Create the 12-Bar Movement Blues:

  1. Divide class into groups of four or five students per group, depending on your class size.
  2. Instruct each group to create different movements for the question and answer sections of the song. For example, the students could clap their hands during the two question phrases and then pat their knees for the answer.
  3. Each group will perform their movements for the class, one group at a time, while the teacher plays the 12-bar-blues progression twice. This allows each group to perform their Movement Blues twice.
  4. Discuss each group's choice of movements and how they worked or did not with the progression. Ask students what, if anything, they would change.

- Backbeat: Explain that in the Rock style, beats 2 and 4 are stressed instead of beats 1 and 3. Ask the students to pat or clap a steady beat in $\frac{4}{4}$. Direct the class to accent the second and fourth clap or pat. This is the backbeat. Play the backbeat on rhythm sticks or claves and the steady beat on drums. Students may trade instruments to allow them to play both the steady beat and the backbeat.

- Put it all together, and help your students to create their own 12-bar blues songs complete with lyrics, a melody, and chords.

Name: _____   Classroom Teacher: _____

Guided Listening Worksheet

Use this worksheet to help you discover musical elements of the piece that your teacher is about to play. Answer each question with as much information as you can while you are listening.

Title: _____   Artist/Composer: _____

Element	Guiding Questions	Your Answers
Rhythm	Do you hear repeated rhythms? Can you identify any rhythmic patterns? Do you hear special rhythmic figures, like syncopation?	
Melody	Does the melody follow a pattern? Can you sketch the contour or shape of the melody?	
Harmony	Do you hear harmony? How many different parts do you hear?	
Form	What is the overall pattern or structure of the music?	
Tone Color	What instruments or voices are making the music? Be as specific as you can.	
Expression	Describe the tempo and dynamics of this music. Are there any big surprises? What is the style of this music?	
Other	What else do you hear or have questions about?	

The original subscriber to *Activate!* has permission to reproduce this page for use in his or her classroom.
© 2009 Heritage Music Press, a division of The Lorenz Corporation. All rights reserved.

Hound Dog
In C

Visual 1
Chord Roots

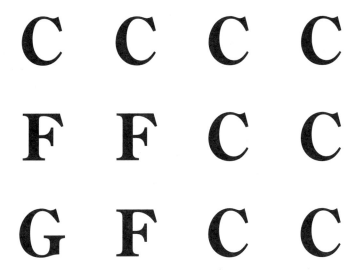

The original subscriber to *Activate!* has permission to reproduce this page for use in his or her classroom.
© 2009 Heritage Music Press, a division of The Lorenz Corporation. All rights reserved.

Hound Dog
In C

Visual 2
Chord Numbers

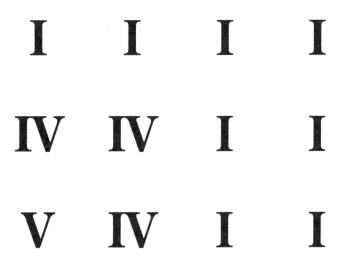

The original subscriber to *Activate!* has permission to reproduce this page for use in his or her classroom.
© 2009 Heritage Music Press, a division of The Lorenz Corporation. All rights reserved.

sleigh ride

Music by Leroy Anderson. Lyrics by Mitchell Parish

Lesson suggestions by Charlene Heldt

Suggested Grades: K–3

Target Concept

Form: Introduction A B A C C' interlude A B A Coda

Materials

- A recording of *Sleigh Ride*
- Icons found in the Data Files on the *Activate!* CD
- Classroom instruments: slapstick, rhythm sticks, jingle bells, maracas
- Icons for grades 2–3

Music-Making Activities

Listening
Playing instruments
Moving to music

 Sleigh Ride Icons

Lesson Suggestions

1. Ask your students if they have ever gone on a sleigh ride.

2. Discuss winter and snow.

3. Tell the class that they are going to listen to a piece called *Sleigh Ride*. Instruct them to raise their hands when they hear the sound of a whip.

4. Play the piece. An instrumental recording is best.

5. Tell the students that there are three distinct musical sections. Invite them to try identifying those sections.

6. While the students are listening, display the icons for the each section. For the older grades, you can simply use letter names to identify the sections.

   Introduction
   A: Sled
   B: Horse
   C and C': Snowflakes
   Interlude
   Coda

7. Listen again, pointing out each section.

8. Divide class into three groups: A, B, and C. Give the first group jingle bells to play on a steady beat during the A section. The second group should play the rhythm sticks during the B section. If you have a slapstick, this is a good time to demonstrate how to play it, letting students take turns. The third should play the maracas during the C and C' sections. You may also want to choose a student "conductor" to point to the icons as the students play along with the recording.

9. If time allows, repeat the activity to allow your students to change instruments.

Extension Activities:

1. Display or distribute lyrics. Have the students sing with the recording. Assign small groups of students to sing specific sections (A, B or C).

2. Divide the class into five groups. Assign each group a section of the piece, (Introduction, A, B, C and Coda) and have them create a movement for their section. Guide this activity as needed. Have the students perform their movements with the recording.

Spotlight on Elvis Presley (1935–1977)

Known as the "King of Rock and Roll"—or sometimes just "the King"—Elvis Aaron Presley was one of the most celebrated and influential musicians of the twentieth century. His songs combined country music from the southern United States with African American gospel and blues in the style that became known as rock and roll. While he did not invent this style, nor was he the first artist to make it popular, Elvis has been called its first real star. His unusual voice, distinctive hairstyle, flashy appearance, and energetic dance moves made him both famous and instantly recognizable around the world. Even today, Elvis continues to hold the record for the largest number of albums sold—more than one billion—and many performers count him among their influences.

Elvis did not have an easy childhood, which is probably one reason that a lot of people related to him and found him so interesting. He was born on January 8, 1935 in his parents' two-room house in Tupelo, Mississippi. He grew up as an only child because his twin brother did not survive. His family was very close, but money was often a problem because his parents had trouble finding and keeping jobs. By the time he was a teenager, Elvis had several jobs to help support his family.

Music was always an important part of Elvis's life. Singing played a central role in the church services that his family attended regularly, his mother shared her love of various musical genres, and he had the opportunity to listen to performances by local country, folk, gospel, and blues musicians. Elvis received his first guitar for his eleventh birthday, when his parents could not afford the bicycle that he had requested. Despite the reason for the gift, it proved to be a good one because he developed his musical talents throughout his school years.

After graduating from high school in 1953, Elvis took a job at a machine shop, but he continued to sing and play the guitar. That summer, he went to the Sun Records Studio in Memphis, Tennessee and paid four dollars to record two songs for his mother's birthday. That session led him to return the next year, when he met studio owner Sam Phillips. Phillips was searching for a performer who could successfully combine qualities of country music with those of rhythm and blues, and he believed that Elvis had the right sound for the job. Their meeting resulted in a record contract, and *That's All Right Mama* became both his first release for Sun Studios and his first regional hit.

Elvis's popularity grew steadily in the years following his first recording with Sun Studios. By 1958, his credits included eleven number one hits—a few them were *Heartbreak Hotel*, *Hound Dog*, and *Jailhouse Rock*—four number one albums, four starring roles in successful movies, and numerous appearances on television programs like the *Ed Sullivan Show*. In that same year, Elvis was drafted into the army. His fans were shocked and worried, but he took his new job seriously and served patriotically. He was stationed in Germany for a year and a half, and then he came home to be part of the Army Reserve until he was discharged in 1964.

Following his time in the army, Elvis continued to record music, to perform, and to act. While his new music did not enjoy the same instant popularity as his earlier hits, he was still seen as a musical legend whose contributions helped to shape rock and roll. When he died in 1977, President Jimmy Carter said that "Elvis Presley's death deprives our country of a part of itself. He was unique and irreplaceable. His music and his personality, fusing the styles of white country and black rhythm and blues, permanently changed the face of American popular culture."

The original subscriber to *Activate!* has permission to reproduce this page for use in his or her classroom.
© 2009 Heritage Music Press, a division of The Lorenz Corporation. All rights reserved.

Spotlight on Ludwig van Beethoven (1770–1827)

Born on December 17, 1770 in the German city of Bonn, Ludwig van Beethoven is one of the most beloved and well-known names in music history. He came from a musical family—his grandfather supervised music and performances for the Elector of Cologne's court in Bonn, and his father, Johann van Beethoven, sang in the Elector's choir and taught the piano and violin—so it is not surprising that his musical education started at a very young age. Ludwig was only fifteen years younger than Wolfgang Amadeus Mozart, who was a very famous child prodigy. Mozart had played the piano for many of the most important people in Europe before he was ten years old, and Johann believed that his son could do the same thing. Some historians have suggested that Johann was a harsh teacher, making his son get up very early and practice the piano until he was exhausted and in tears.

Ludwig also studied piano and composition with a number of local musicians, and he showed a great deal of talent. His most important teacher was the Cologne court organist, Christian Gottlob Neefe. Neefe recognized and encouraged Ludwig's many musical skills, teaching him with the piano, the organ, and the viola. With Neefe's assistance, Ludwig learned to improvise very complicated piano melodies, and he published his first three piano sonatas. As his talents and reputation grew, many people compared his promise with that of the young Mozart.

In 1787, Ludwig traveled to Vienna, Austria so that he could take lessons from Mozart himself. Most historians believe that he succeeded in this goal, but he was only able to stay in Vienna for about two weeks. Then, he received news from his family that his mother was sick. She died shortly after he returned to Bonn, and Ludwig took a job teaching piano lessons to help support his family. He taught and worked on his compositions for several years, and then returned to Vienna to study with Franz Joseph Haydn.

Ludwig was a very different kind of composer than Mozart or Haydn, who each wrote hundreds of pieces of music. Looking only at the numbers, Ludwig's nine symphonies, thirty-two piano sonatas, sixteen string quartets, and assorted other compositions for solos and small groups of instruments seem like a small amount of music to fill an entire career. However, his compositions were longer and more complex than the music of earlier times. His style bridged the Classical and Romantic periods, combining Classical forms, order, and elegance with a new kind of extended musical development that explored intense emotions and intricate musical ideas. Composing did not come easily to Ludwig. Instead, he had to work and rework his melodies and harmonies until the sound matched exactly what he had imagined.

When Ludwig was only twenty-four years old, he learned that he was losing his hearing. His doctors told him that there was no cure and that, eventually, he would be entirely deaf. Learning that he would lose so much contact with the world along with the music that he loved caused him to become very depressed, but he did not give up. Instead, he continued to compose and captured many of his own emotions in his works. Some of the stories say that he pounded on piano keys just to feel the vibrations in the floor. His obvious love of music made him an artistic hero even in his own time.

In spite of his many difficulties, Ludwig van Beethoven left behind a musical legacy that few have been able to match. Such great composers as Brahms, Mahler, Mendelssohn, and Wagner all compared their works against his and wondered whether they would be able to live up to his greatness.

The original subscriber to *Activate!* has permission to reproduce this page for use in his or her classroom.
© 2009 Heritage Music Press, a division of The Lorenz Corporation. All rights reserved.

Name: _____   Classroom Teacher: _____

Beethoven Meets... Elvis?

Would you have ever guessed that Ludwig van Beethoven and Elvis Presley had a lot in common?
Test your knowledge with these questions.

1. At only eleven years old, who showed enough musical talent to work as his teacher's assistant?

 Beethoven   Elvis    Both

2. Which musician was a teenager when he first took a job to help support his family?

 Beethoven   Elvis    Both

3. Who is remembered as a kind of hero for overcoming life's difficulties and making memorable and important music?

 Beethoven   Elvis    Both

4. Who received his first musical instrument when his parents couldn't afford the birthday present that he really wanted?

 Beethoven    Elvis    Both

5. Compared to others from the same time, this musician had fewer pieces of music to his name even though they were much longer and more complex.

 Beethoven    Elvis    Both

6. Who famously put together a performance for his mother's birthday, which also led to his successful musical career?

 Beethoven    Elvis    Both

7. Who is famous for taking musical ideas that had been around for a long time and combining them to create something entirely new?

 Beethoven    Elvis    Both

The original subscriber to *Activate!* has permission to reproduce this page for use in his or her classroom.
© 2009 Heritage Music Press, a division of The Lorenz Corporation. All rights reserved.

Name: _____   Classroom Teacher: _____

8. Who loved music so much that he found ways to continue his career even after he started losing his hearing?

 Beethoven    Elvis    Both

9. Who interrupted his musical career to serve in the army?

 Beethoven   Elvis    Both

10. Whose music was popular during his own life and whose musical reputation has only grown since his death?

 Beethoven   Elvis    Both

11. Which musician left behind such a powerful legacy that composers and performers today still count him among their most important influences?

 Beethoven   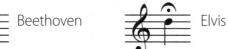 Elvis   Both

Bonus

Arrange the notes and rests from each answer in order, on the staff below. Use a recorder or other classroom instrument to play through the melody. What is the name of this famous piece of music?

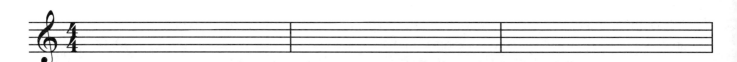

_____

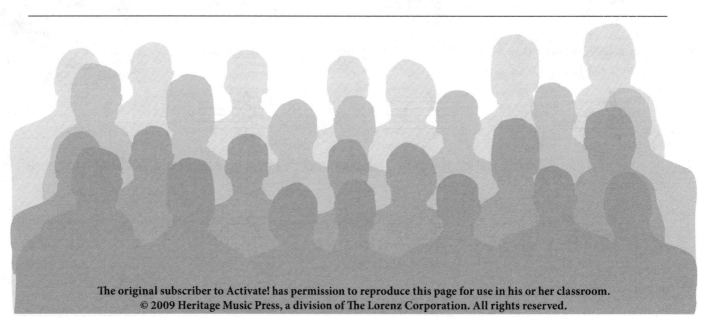

The original subscriber to Activate! has permission to reproduce this page for use in his or her classroom.
© 2009 Heritage Music Press, a division of The Lorenz Corporation. All rights reserved.

Name: _____   Classroom Teacher: _____

Musical Ornament

Here is your chance to design a personalized musical ornament for yourself or someone else. Just follow the directions and use the musical code below to turn a name (your own or another special person's) into a melody.

1. Write a name on the line below. You can use your name or someone else's:

    _____

2. Now, spell the name using the following musical alphabet code. (H becomes A, I becomes B, etc.)

A	**B**	**C**	**D**	**E**	**F**	**G**
H	I	J	K	L	M	N
O	P	Q	R	S	T	U
V	W	X	Y	Z		

    Write the new musical name on the line provided: _____

3. Compose a melody using the pitches of your musical name on the music staff inside the ornament below. Be sure to select a time signature and appropriate rhythm values. You can even perform the new composition on your favorite instrument!

4. Cut out the ornament, decorate it, punch a small hole, attach some string and you have a simple gift to share.

The original subscriber to *Activate!* has permission to reproduce this page for use in his or her classroom.
© 2009 Heritage Music Press, a division of The Lorenz Corporation. All rights reserved.

Name: _____   Classroom Teacher: _____

Candy Cane Caper!

Directions: The Christmas Elves need help getting the candy canes in the correct stocking. Write the number of beats (not notes) in each blank. Then, cut out all of the pieces, turn them over, and play a game of memory by matching the stocking and candy cane that have the same number of beats.

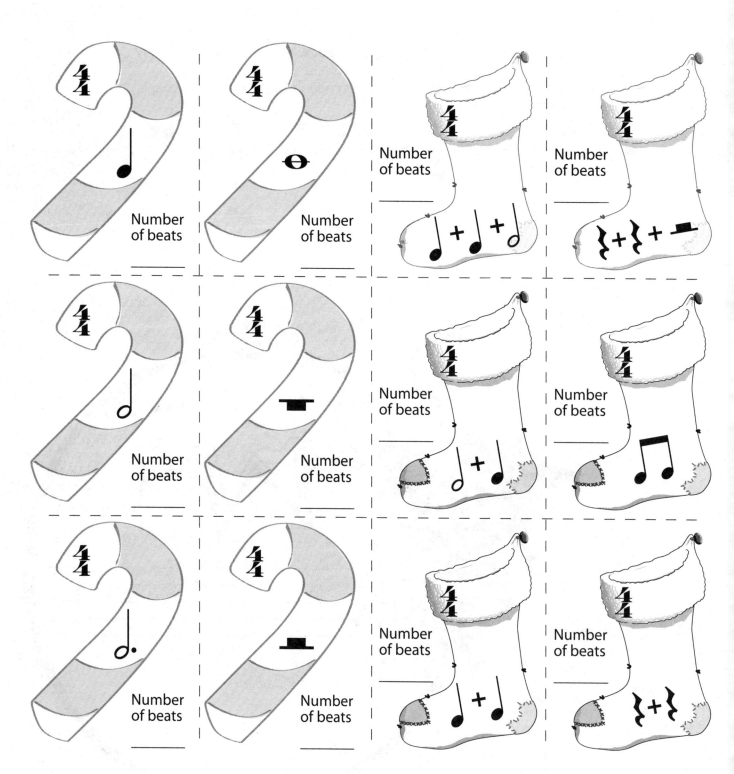

The original subscriber to *Activate!* has permission to reproduce this page for use in his or her classroom.
© 2009 Heritage Music Press, a division of The Lorenz Corporation. All rights reserved.

Over the River . . .

Directions: Follow the musical alphabet through the maze. Beginning at the Start, draw a path between each of the musical pitch names until you reach the Finish at the end of the maze. Remember the musical pitches are; A, B, C, D, E, F, G. Just like in a melody, they do not have to be in alphabetical order though.

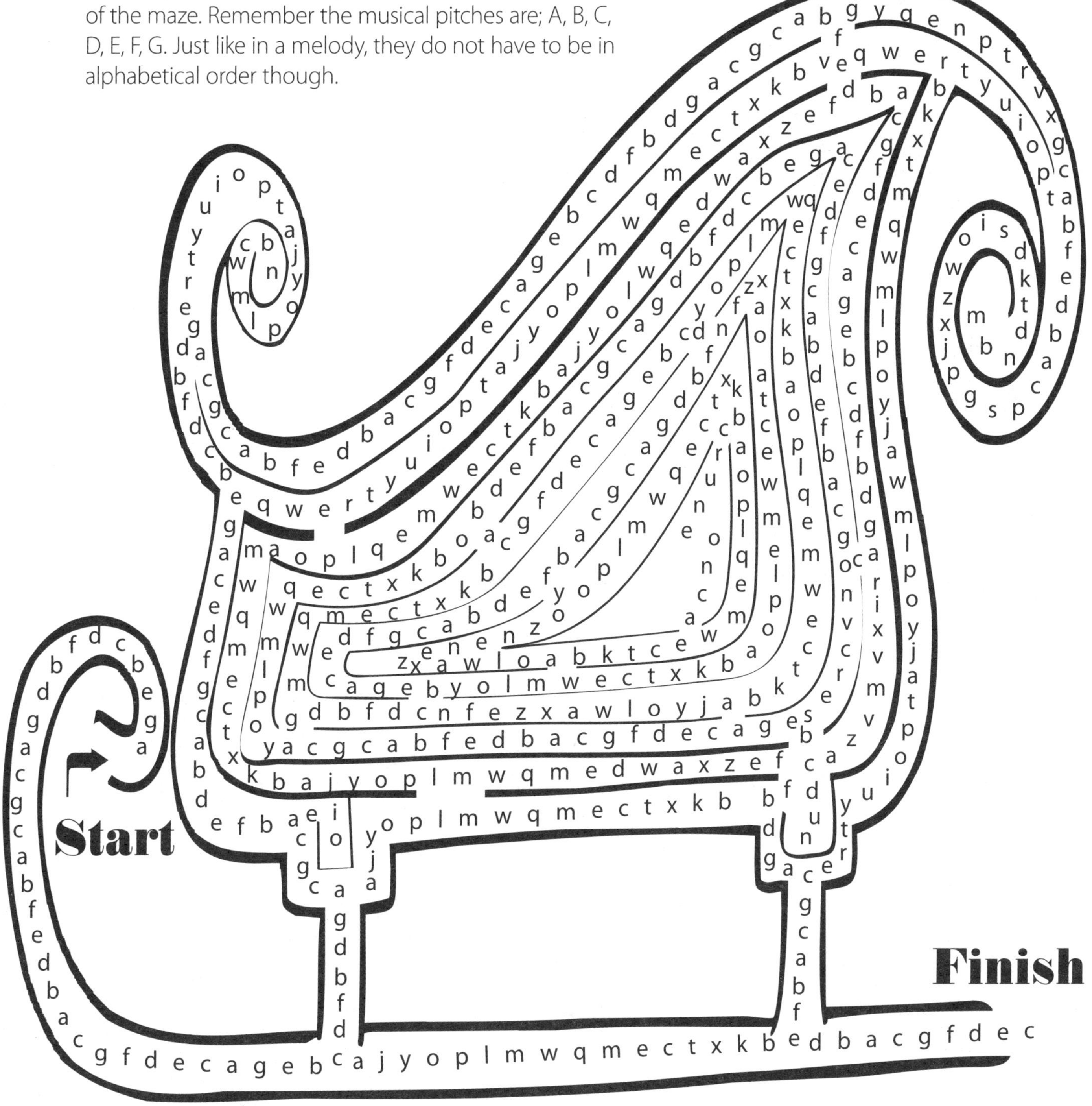

Start

Finish

The original subscriber to *Activate!* has permission to reproduce this page for use in his or her classroom.
© 2009 Heritage Music Press, a division of The Lorenz Corporation. All rights reserved.

Name: _____   Classroom Teacher: _____

Name that Tune! Elvis Presley

Directions: Elvis Presley's birthday is January 8th. Help us celebrate by figuring out the names to some of his most famous songs. Use the clues below to decode the song titles. Write the title in the blank below each example.

1. B +  – G  –N + – NEL +S

Title: _____

2.  +

Title: _____

3. – B   S + ↑

Title: _____

4. 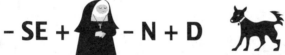 – SE + – N + D

Title: _____

5. L + – D   M + – YE – T + – E

Title: _____

6.  – U  – E – A + – F

Title: _____

The original subscriber to *Activate!* has permission to reproduce this page for use in his or her classroom.
© 2009 Heritage Music Press, a division of The Lorenz Corporation. All rights reserved.

Name: _____   Classroom Teacher: _____

WINTER RHYTHMS

Directions: Look carefully at the rhythm in each snowflake. Say each rhythm in your head. Match each rhythm to the word or phrase that has the same number of sounds (syllables) by drawing a line to connect them. The first one has been done for you. Can you make a winter rhythm rap using some of these words?

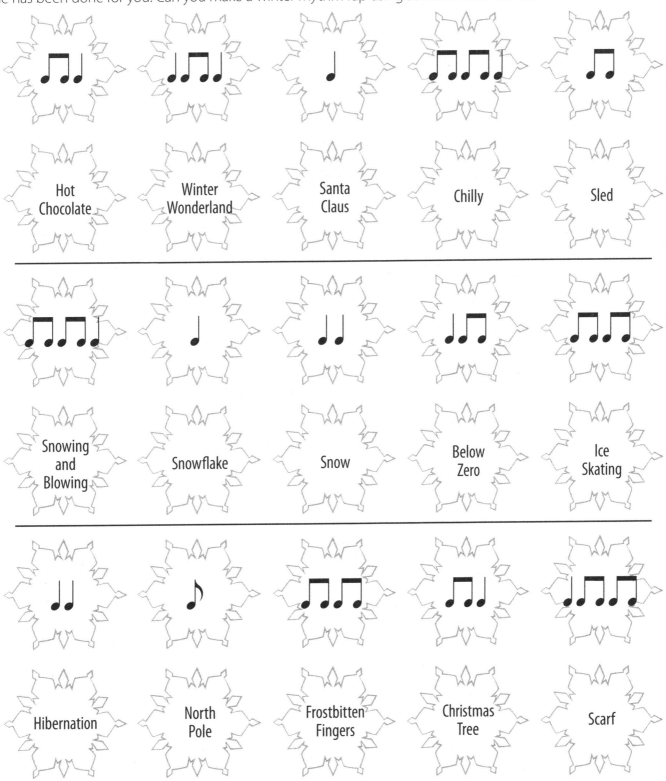

Hot Chocolate

Winter Wonderland

Santa Claus

Chilly

Sled

Snowing and Blowing

Snowflake

Snow

Below Zero

Ice Skating

Hibernation

North Pole

Frostbitten Fingers

Christmas Tree

Scarf

The original subscriber to *Activate!* has permission to reproduce this page for use in his or her classroom.
© 2009 Heritage Music Press, a division of The Lorenz Corporation. All rights reserved.

Name: _____ Classroom Teacher: _____

Color By Rhythm

Directions: color each note or rest in the picture below with the following colors.

ꝿ = White	⦚ = Brown	= Dark Blue	♪ = Orange					
♩ = Green	♩ = Red	o = Gray	♫ = Purple	♬ = Light Blue				

The original subscriber to *Activate!* has permission to reproduce this page for use in his or her classroom.
© 2009 Heritage Music Press, a division of The Lorenz Corporation. All rights reserved.

Name: _____   Classroom Teacher: _____

Harmonious Holidays

 22-29

Directions: Listen to each musical example. Decide if the music is just a melody or if you hear a melody with harmony. Circle the word "melody" if you hear only the melody or circle "harmony" if you hear a melody with a harmony. Remember harmony means you hear more than one musical pitch at a time.

1. Jingle Bells   melody   harmony

2. Deck the Hall   melody   harmony

3. Greensleeves   melody   harmony

4. Over the River   melody   harmony

5. Good King Wenceslas   melody   harmony

6. Up on the House Top   melody   harmony

7. We Wish You A Merry Christmas   melody   harmony

8. Silent Night   melody   harmony

The original subscriber to *Activate!* has permission to reproduce this page for use in his or her classroom.
© 2009 Heritage Music Press, a division of The Lorenz Corporation. All rights reserved.

Name: _____ Classroom Teacher: _____

A Caroling Crossword

Directions: Complete the crossword puzzle below using the clues at the bottom of the page. Each clue is part of a famous Christmas Carol. Fill in the puzzle with the title of each carol.

Across

4. "Of all the trees within the wood, the holly bears the crown."
5. "Please to put a penny in an old man's hat."
9. "When the snow lay round a-bout,"
10. "Troll the ancient Yuletide carol,"
11. "Joyful all ye nations rise,"

Down

1. "Now bring us some figgy pudding."
2. "The horse knows the way to carry the sleigh,"
3. "…out jumps good ol' Santa Claus!"
6. "…seven swans a swimming…"
7. "Dashing through the snow,"
8. "…among the leaves so green."

The original subscriber to *Activate!* has permission to reproduce this page for use in his or her classroom.
© 2009 Heritage Music Press, a division of The Lorenz Corporation. All rights reserved.

Answer Keys

Page 67
Beethoven Meets...Elvis?

1. Beethoven
2. Both
3. Both
4. Elvis
5. Beethoven
6. Elvis
7. Both
8. Beethoven
9. Elvis
10. Both
11. Both

The melody should be the first two measure of Beethoven's Fifth Symphony.

Page 70
Candy Cane Caper

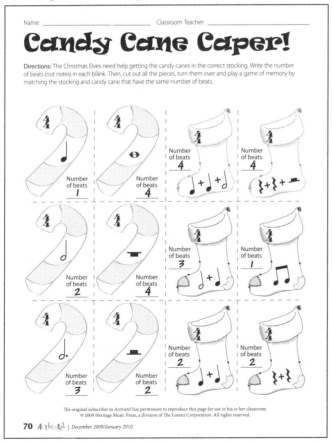

The original subscriber to *Activate!* has permission to reproduce this page for use in his or her classroom.
© 2009 Heritage Music Press, a division of The Lorenz Corporation. All rights reserved.

Page 71
Over the River

The original subscriber to *Activate!* has permission to reproduce this page for use in his or her classroom.
© 2009 Heritage Music Press, a division of The Lorenz Corporation. All rights reserved.

Page 72
Name That Tune!

1. Blue Suede Shoes
2. Jailhouse Rock
3. All Shook Up
4. Hound Dog
5. Love Me Tender
6. Don't Be Cruel

Answer Keys

Page 73
Winter Rhythms

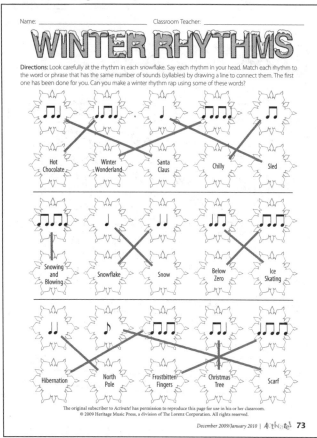

Page 74
Color By Rhythm

Page 75
Harmonious Holidays

1. Harmony
2. Melody
3. Harmony
4. Harmony
5. Melody
6. Melody
7. Melody
8. Harmony

Page 76
A Caroling Crossword

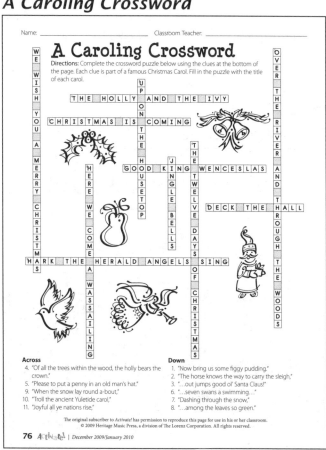

National Standards for Music Education Index

Plus reproducible student parts are provided for most of the songs in "Ready, Set, Sing" and "Ready, Set, Play."

Plus full-version recordings are provided of most of the songs in "Ready, Set, Sing," "Ready, Set, Play" and "Ready, Set, Move."

National Standards for Music Education Index

From *National Standards for Arts Education*. © 1994 by Music Educators National Conference (MENC). Used by permission. The complete National Arts Standards and additional materials relating to the Standards are available from MENC—The National Association for Music Education, 1806 Robert Fulton Drive, Reston, VA 20191.

Statement of Ownership, Management and Circulation
(Required by 39 U. S. C. 3685)

1. Publication Title: Activate!
2. Publication Number: 1931-4736
3. Filing Date: September 8, 2009
4. Issue Frequency: Bi-monthly, except June and July
5. Number of Issues Published Annually: 5
6. Annual Subscription Price: $64.95
7. Office of Publication *(Not printer)*: 501 E. Third St., P.O. Box 802, Dayton, Montgomery County, OH 45401–0802, U.S.A.
8. General Business Office *(Not printer)*: 501 E. Third St., P.O. Box 802, Dayton, Montgomery County, OH 45401–0802, U.S.A.
9. Publisher: Lorenz Publishing Co., 501 E. Third St., P.O. Box 802, Dayton, Montgomery County, OH 45401–0802, U.S.A.
   Editor: Kris Kropff, 501 E. Third St., P.O. Box 802, Dayton, Montgomery County, OH 45401–0802, U.S.A.
   Managing Editor: Larry Pugh, 501 E. Third St., P.O. Box 802, Dayton, Montgomery County, OH 45401–0802, U.S.A.
10. Owner: Lorenz Publishing Company, Reiff Lorenz, President, 501 E. Third St., P.O. Box 802, Dayton, Montgomery County, OH 45401–0802, U.S.A.
11. Bondholders: None
13. Activate!
14. Issue Date for Circulation Data Below: August/September 2009

15. Extent and Nature of Circulation

	Average No. Copies Each Issue During Preceding 12 months	No. Copies of Single Issue Published Nearest to Filing Date
a. Total Number of Copies *(Net press run)*	3,457	3,086
b. Paid and/or Requested Circulation		
1. Paid/Requested Outside-County Mail Subscriptions Stated on Form 3541	2,483	1,857
2. Paid In-Country Subscriptions Stated on Form 3541	5	0
3. Sales Through Dealers and Carriers, Street Venders, Counter Sales, and Other Non-USPS Paid Distribution	644	1,000
4. Other Classes Mailed Through the USPS	47	36
c. Total Paid and/or Requested Circulation *[Sum of 15b. (1), (2), (3), and (4)]*	3,179	2,893
d. Free Distribution by Mail *(Samples, complimentary, and other free)*		
1. Outside-County as Stated on Form 3541	0	0
2. In-County as Stated on Form 3541	0	0
3. Other Classes Mailed Through the USPS	0	0
4. Free Distribution Outside the Mail *(Carriers or other means)*	77	58
e. Total Free Distribution *(Sum of 15d. and 15e.)*	77	58
f. Total Distribution (sum of 15c. & 15f.)	3,256	2,951
g. Copies not Distributed	201	135
h. Total (sum of 15g. & h.)	3,457	3,086
i. Percent Paid and/or Requested Circulation *(15c. divided by 15g. times 100)*	91.9%	98%

16. Publication of Statement of Ownership will be printed in the December 2009/January 2010 issue of this publication.
17. Signature and Title of Editor, Publisher, Business Manager, or Owner
    Date: September 8, 2009

I certify that all information furnished on this form is true and complete. I understand that anyone who furnishes false or misleading information on this form or who omits material or information requested on the form may be subject to criminal sanctions (including fines and imprisonment) and/or civil sanctions (including civil penalties).

Reiff Lorenz, President